Parents and Professionals in Early Childhood Settings

Parents and Professionals in Early Childhood Settings

Glenda Mac Naughton
Patrick Hughes

Open University Press

Open University Press
McGraw-Hill Education
McGraw-Hill House
Shoppenhangers Road
Maidenhead
Berkshire
England
SL6 2QL

email: enquiries@openup.co.uk
world wide web: www.openup.co.uk

and Two Penn Plaza, New York, NY 10121-2289, USA

First published 2011

A catalogue record of this book is available from the British Library

ISBN-13: 978-0-33-524373-0 (pb)
ISBN-10: 0-33-524378-8 (pb)
eISBN: 978-0-33-524374-7

Library of Congress Cataloging-in-Publication Data
CIP data applied for

Typeset by RefineCatch Limited, Bungay, Suffolk
Printed in the UK by Ashford Colour Press Ltd., Gosport, Hants.

Fictitious names of companies, products, people, characters and/or data that may be used
herein (in case studies or in examples) are not intended to represent any real individual,
company, product or event.

The McGraw·Hill Companies

Contents

Acknowledgements   vi
Preface   vii
Introduction   ix

1   We/they are always available . . . but in snatches of time   1
2   Understanding the professional   12
3   Revealing ignorance   23
4   Joining in – the benefits and costs   35
5   We speak English here   46
6   We respect 'their' culture   57
7   Disclosing personal details – who needs to know?   68
8   Welcoming parents . . . but not really in this space   81
9   Ways to communicate . . . but don't ruffle their feathers   91
10   I just want some feedback!   103
11   She'll love the sausage sizzle!   113
12   I'm learning how to teach my child to read   125
13   They're just not involved   137
14   Boys who like to be different   148
15   Lesbian mums – what's the fuss?   160
16   Are we genuine partners and how do we know?   173
17   That's jargon to me!   185

Appendices
1   A Fairness Alerts Matrix   198
2   Summaries of the major research projects on which the book is based   202
3   A quick guide to the book's research sources   205
4   Handouts for classes, meetings, discussions, newsletters and noticeboards   210
5   Glossary of key terms   215

Index   218

Acknowledgements

Throughout this book, we draw on the experiences of the parents, early childhood education and care staff and students with whom we have worked over many years. We thank them for their generosity in sharing their experiences and perspectives with us and, through this book, with others. We have worked with them in research projects conducted through the Centre for Equity and Innovation in Early Childhood (CEIEC), which is situated in the University of Melbourne's Graduate School of Education. Glenda Mac Naughton was the Foundation Director of the CEIEC and Patrick Hughes a Research Fellow of the CEIEC.

Many CEIEC staff and postgraduate students participated in our research projects and we thank them all for their support and encouragement. Special thanks go to our CEIEC colleagues Dr Kylie Smith and Ms Kate Alexander, who in their own way have been crucial to the success of our work.

Throughout this book, we have referred to our research participants only by pseudonyms, unless they have requested otherwise, in line with the University of Melbourne's Human Research Ethics Committee protocols. We detail the major projects on which this book draws in *Appendix 2*.

Preface

Many 'Western', industrialised societies expect that families and early childhood staff will collaborate in the education and care of young children. Such collaboration is referred to in different ways including:

- parent and/or family involvement
- parent and/or family participation
- parent and/or family engagement
- parent and/or family partnerships
- parent and/or family collaboration
- learning communities
- family-based **or** family-centred practices
- community building.

Early childhood education and care staff can find ample professional advice about how to promote parent involvement in their services. However, much of that advice has no grounding in the daily lives of staff and families. Instead, it prescribes an established menu of activities, of which these appear most often:

- meetings – formal and informal
- newsletters
- communication books
- notice-boards
- open days
- fundraising events.

Such activities certainly *can* help to create and shape relationships between staff and families, but only rarely do they respond to what staff and families *say* about their relationships.

We have been researching relationships between staff and parents in early childhood settings for 10 years and participants in our research certainly knew that menu of activities. However, few of our participants – parents and staff – had found the items on the menu useful as they sought common ground around complex, difficult and sometimes controversial issues, such as bereavement, food/diet preferences, circumcision, challenging behaviour, discrimination and bullying. They also said that finding common ground is harder when there are different perspectives on a particular issue, when staff and families had dissimilar backgrounds and experiences and when unspoken issues of power and knowledge made it hard to collaborate in ethical and equitable ways. As if this was not enough, staff and families also told us consistently that in most early childhood settings, there just is not the time and space needed to explore and resolve these issues. That menu addresses none of these problems.

In these circumstances, it is no surprise that relationships between staff and families in early childhood settings are often marked by doubt, uncertainty, frustration and mistrust. When those relationships do not work, each side feels guilty, stressed and distressed. Remarkably, however, many staff and families in our research projects remained hopeful that with goodwill, space and time they could forge respectful, meaningful and mutually supportive relationships.

We have written *Parents and professionals in early childhood settings* as a resource for early childhood staff, students, academics and trainers and for parents and other carers of young children. Rather than recycling that set menu of 'things you should do', it addresses the 'real' issues that 'real' staff and families have told us they face daily.

Our target readers are:

- The early childhood academy (academics, undergraduate students and postgraduate students). The book would be useful at all levels of undergraduate courses, as chapters could be used selectively to introduce students to specific issues. It could be a set text for Honours programmes and for coursework Master's degrees.
- The early childhood field (early childhood teachers, childcare staff, family day care staff, managers, trainers). The book will be both a resource and an inspiration for people in this field who wish to create and sustain respectful and equitable relationships with parents and other carers, but are unsure how best to do so.
- The early childhood policy arena (advocates, policy-makers, advisers and administrators, including those working in the early years of schooling). These readers can use the book as a source of 'case studies' of staff–parent relationships to assist them to create and enact equitable policies concerning the care and education of young children.
- Parents and carers of young children. Much of the literature around parent–staff relationships is directed at staff and aims to improve their ability to communicate effectively with the parents and carers with whom they work. However, communication is always interactive, with each side needing to understand the other's position. This book contributes to that mutual understanding.

Introduction

Parents and professionals in early childhood settings is written for the diverse people who make up the field of early childhood education and care. They include staff, students, academics, trainers, curriculum advisers, policy officers and managers, together with the parents and other carers of young children.

Some readers will read the book from start to finish, but it has been written so that readers can read each chapter separately, as a particular issue emerges in their specific setting, service or circumstance. Each chapter starts with a story[1] that we have built from our research into relationships between staff and families. Each story captures the various understandings, desires and feelings about an issue as expressed by parents, staff and children and is written in a lively and accessible style to engage a diverse readership. Each story features the voices and perspectives of 'real' staff and families in our research. Each one illustrates a complex, difficult and/or controversial issue and highlights the questions of power and knowledge surrounding that issue.

The stories that open each chapter reflect our use in our research of 'little narratives', a term originated – *'petit recits'* – by Jean-Francois Lyotard, a French theorist of postmodernity (see, for example, MacNaughton and Hughes, 2000: MacNaughton and Hughes, 2001; MacNaughton and Hughes, 2008). As staff and families in our research studies (see Appendix 2 for details) co-authored 'little narratives' about complex, difficult and/or controversial issues arising from their shared daily contact with children, they asked new questions about those issues, created new ideas about them and generated new rules about how to discuss them. In turn – and to different extents – creating 'little narratives' changed relationships between them: from 'experts and non-experts' they became 'co-authors'. 'Little narratives' do not aim necessarily to create or reflect consensus. Rather, they aim to create dissensus or disagreement, because this is more likely than agreement to provoke change. It is in our disagreements or dissensus that we question the dominant ideas, beliefs, norms and values and seek to change them. The 'little narratives'

---

[1] In some chapters where a story focuses on meetings between parents and practitioners the names of the parents have been italicized to enable you to differentiate between the two groups.

can then be shared with others through, for example, centre newsletters, staff–parent discussions and group meetings, with the aim of recruiting more co-authors continuously.

The stories in this book can be used as case studies of particular issues or controversies by academics and trainers (pre-service and post-service) and by small groups or whole teams of staff and/or parents; and individuals can use them as points of reflection.

Each chapter's opening story is supported as follows:

- Key terms are highlighted in the text, then collected into a Glossary in Appendix 5.
- 'Research Snippets' invite readers to reflect critically on the issues raised in the story.
- 'Fairness Alerts' introduce readers to unfair thinking habits that often emerge in discussions about the issues raised in the story, explain why they are unfair and advise readers how to challenge them.
- 'Models of staff–parent relationships' around the issues raised in the story encourage readers to look at an issue from more than one perspective.
- 'Points to Ponder' and 'Points to Discuss' encourage readers – individually and in groups – to extend their thinking about the issues raised in the story.
- Annotated 'Further reading' encourages readers to develop their understandings of the issues raised in the story.

The 'Research Snippets' in each chapter are drawn from relevant international research about staff–parent relationships in early childhood education and care settings, including schools. The language used to describe these services for young children varies between countries and the same word (e.g. 'kindergarten') can refer to services for children between 3 and 8 years of age. For this reason, if a Research Snippet does not specify the age of any children involved, readers should note its country of origin and refer to the Glossary to identify the children's likely age range. Most of the published research available in English language journals is from the USA, but wherever we can, we have also drawn on research from other countries. We provide full bibliographic details of each Research Snippet, so that readers can access the full text if they wish.

The book's 'Fairness Alerts' draw on poststructuralist and postcolonial approaches to the politics of knowledge. Each Fairness Alert shows how particular habits of thinking can lead to unjust relationships between early childhood staff and parents. In our work with parents and staff, we have identified six unfair thinking habits:

1   essentializing
2   homogenizing
3   othering
4   privileging
5   silencing.

Each chapter introduces at least one of these unfair thinking habits and shows how it works, why it is unfair, and how to challenge it. We argue that staff and parents can build fairer relationships with each other as they see, hear and understand what is just and unjust in their thinking habits and, as a result, build fairer habits of thinking about each other. Appendix 1 – *A Fairness Alerts Matrix* – summarizes the book's Fairness Alerts.

The five unfair thinking habits are not always mutually exclusive. For example, when you 'privilege' a certain idea or approach, you can 'homogenize' anyone who disagrees with you into 'the other' and 'silence' them. However, such slippage between unfair thinking habits does not always happen and introducing each one individually highlights particular elements or characteristics that may be lost or confused if two or more are introduced simultaneously.

In each chapter we also draw on the international early childhood research and professional literature to present two models of staff–parent relationships that are found commonly in discussions and research around the issues in the chapter's opening story. It is rare for writers and researchers to identify the model/s underpinning their work. Instead, models must be teased out through a critical reading of the work, showing how its author's approach to an issue expresses their model of how people behave with each other. For example, an author's approach to parents' role in literacy may focus on the significance of professional expertise or, in contrast, it may focus on the significance of a child's surroundings.

Finally, each chapter features several 'Points to Ponder' and 'Points to Discuss'. Their purpose is to encourage readers – individually and in groups – to think about whether and how the issues raised in the story are relevant to their particular circumstances, rather than just repeat a menu of 'things we should do' that, as we have found in our research, may or may not work in particular circumstances.

Our intention in this book is to bring the struggles, insights, experiences, and voices of parents and staff centre stage in discussions about their relationships. So often, parents and staff are targets of advice that ignores the material and cultural realities they face in creating and sustaining relationships with each other. In many countries, the material realities for staff consist of poor working conditions that make staff time-poor, underpaid and inadequately prepared for relationships with parents, while being expected to solve all that is wrong with a society. Expectations that early childhood education and care will reduce the prison population, improve a nation's literacy and build a more productive workforce are evident in much of the research literature on parent involvement. Alongside this, in many countries the material realities for parents and carers consist of a lack of family-friendly work policies and practices that sap their time and energy for parent involvement in early childhood education and care settings. Staff and parents also face the realities of building relationships among cultural differences (in, for example, their values, experiences, expectations, child-rearing practices, rituals and traditions) associated with their age, place of birth, immigration experiences, socio-economic status, sexuality, language, religion, ability and gender.

We have learnt through the generous involvement of staff and parents in our research and that of other researchers internationally that what is expected of them among these material and cultural realities is neither easy nor simple. It is our hope this book inspires discussions and practices that support staff and parents in their efforts to create and sustain fair, respectful, realistic and meaningful relationships with each other.

References

MacNaughton, G. and Hughes, P. (2000) Consensus, dissensus or community: the politics of parent involvement in early childhood education. *Contemporary Issues in Early Childhood*, 1(3): 241–58.

MacNaughton, G. and Hughes, P. (2001) Early childhood professionals learning to work with parents: the challenges of diversity and dissensus. *Australian Journal of Early Childhood*, 26(4): 32–8.

MacNaughton, G. and Hughes, P. (2008) Whose truth do you privilege? Parents, partnerships and power, in F. Degraff and A. Van Keulen (eds) *Making the Road As We Go: Parents and Professions as Partners Managing Diversity in Early Childhood*. The Netherlands, SWP Publishing: 74–84.

1   We/they are always available
   . . . but in snatches of time

The story

To help you quickly grasp who's who, practitioners' names are shown in upright font and parents' names are shown in *italic* font.

Staff and parents at the TreeTops Centre have said, in different ways, that there is never enough time during the day for a good discussion. In response, the Centre is holding its first 'Staff and Parents Evening' to enable such discussions to happen. Lots of parents and staff have attended and formed small groups in different corners. The room is buzzing! One group has two staff – Abbey and Julia – and four parents – *Damien, Aretha, Kaye* and *Shayna*.

Abbey: You know, don't you, that you can speak to me at any time about anything that might be worrying you or that might have happened at home. I'm always happy to listen.

Julia: Yeah, that's the same for me, too. If there's something worrying you – about your children, or whatever – do please come and tell me about it.

Damien: Yes, you're always willing to listen to us, which is great, but there never seems to be a good time to talk, because you're always so busy with the kids, or sometimes we have to rush off somewhere else.

Abbey: But I wish we had more time to do that. There's never enough time in the day to do everything, is there, Julia?

Julia: Oh, tell me about it! Time's tight so often. Actually, lack of time's a bit of a thing with me. I feel dreadful because I can only talk to parents in snatches of time between doing everything else. It makes it hard to get to know them, you know?

Aretha: I know you're always willing to listen but, yes, it's timing. You know, when you get here, the kids are all sort of rushing in and you always seem to find some other mother talking about something. I don't like to hold up the session as it begins, because I think it's the kids' time. And I'm sort of standing there, waiting and waiting until it's my time for a chat. So I don't say anything, or the session won't get started for 20 minutes and the kids miss out and after the session it's sort of all happening again.

Damien: It would be great if we could just have even fifteen minutes at the end of the session.

Kaye: And this evening's a really good idea. It would be great if we could have one of these every so often.

Aretha: Yes, but we've got to remember that all these bits of extra time, they're in the staff's own time, outside of work, and it doesn't seem fair that they have to do this.

Julia: Oh well, it gives me a break from the housework! (Laughter) But you know that I'll always make time if you want to come and talk.

Aretha: Well, yes, but it's like snatching time out of the chaos and when you do, you just feel – well, I feel – a bit awkward because you know that something else should be happening. So like you said, Julia, it's hard to get to know someone in that situation. But I guess that's just how it is.

Shayna: It's always sort of rushed . . . when you get here it's rushed and when you're leaving, um, you can sort of sense that the staff are tired and there is too much going on. You encourage us to talk to you at any point, but lots of times I've waited until it's my turn, but you're sort of at the tail end and the kids are running out there. . . . I know probably if I wanted to ring and make an appointment to see someone I could, but I wouldn't unless I really had to. I would sort of operate within the boundaries of what's there.

Kaye: I mean, the best chance you can get to talk to staff is when you're working, but then you're sort of half looking at the other children. . . . You can't always give full attention to what we're talking about and what we're asking, but you're doing your job, so we have to just sort of make the best of it, I suppose.

Julia: Well, you shouldn't have to, really, but I don't know what we can do about it. We're all pretty much in the same boat.

Abbey: I'm not sure that's always true, Julia. In my last centre, we had lots of families from different cultures – from Somalia, Cambodia. And some knew their way around and could speak English pretty well, so they were quite easy to talk to and we had some good talks. But the others – especially if they hadn't been here long – couldn't figure out how everything worked and didn't have much English. And they needed some more support than the others, and I tried to support them a bit, but I couldn't do much, really – there weren't enough hours in the day. So I felt bad about that and I was concerned about them. And I worked at that centre for three years, but I never really learnt much about those other cultures, because there was never a chance to just sit down and talk to them. So I felt bad about that, too! (Laughter)

Aretha: Well, I have to say that it can be hard for people who aren't, you know, 'Anglo-Australian' to feel that we're on that 'level playing field'. For example, my family's background is partly Mauritian and partly Anglo-Indian and at home we try to make sure that our kids learn about those different cultures and see things from them. But often in centres and **kindergartens** – and I'm not getting at anyone *here* – but you don't see much about specific cultures. Everything's just, sort of, massed together.

Julia: But that's not happening here, is it? We have our special Italian Day when the kids eat pasta and our Greek Day when they get kebabs. And Abbey's always bringing in different sorts of music and we do, you know, the 'Zorba the Greek' dancing.

Kaye: And I guess that doing things like that is just even more work for you, isn't it? And it's great that you do it, but I guess those multicultural parents might think, 'Oh well, they're doing their best, we can't really ask for anything special.'

Resources for thinking and talking about staff–parent relationships

Research Snippets

Here are two snippets from the research concerning the importance of time for quality communication between parents and staff in **early childhood education and care** settings. Research Snippet 1 is taken from a study of staff–parent communication in childcare centres in the USA (Kennedy Reedy and Hobbins McGrath, 2008: 354) and it echoes *Shayna*'s and *Kate*'s complaints that it can be hard to find time to talk with staff. A study of childcare in Ireland (Martin, 2003) found similar difficulties and a summary of some of its key findings forms Research Snippet 2.

Following each Research Snippet are some 'Points to Ponder' and some 'Points to Discuss', which may help you decide whether you agree that staff–parent communication in linguistically and ethnically diverse settings is a matter of 'just sort of (making) the best of it, I suppose' (*Kaye*, in the story).

Research Snippet 1: Can you hear me now? Staff–parent communication in child care centres (Kennedy Reedy and Hobbins McGrath, 2008)

Kennedy Reedy and Hobbins McGrath (2008) report on two case studies of staff–parent communication in childcare centres in the USA. Case study one consisted of interviews with 11 directors of childcare centres; case study two was a 12-month-long ethnographic study of parents in a childcare centre.

Some key findings

- Staff and parents recognize that establishing positive and effective communication between them is a major challenge.
- Communication between staff and parents happens most often at drop-off and pick-up, that is times that are often fraught for both staff and parents.

If teachers are to address parents' concerns, then they need support and training in parent relations. By the end of the day both teachers and parents feel depleted, yet it is often at pick-up time that the greatest sensitivity is needed to brainstorm creative and effective solutions to behavioural concerns. Parents and teachers have a different rhythm to their days, making end-of-the-day impromptu conferences stressful for teachers and unsatisfying for parents. If pick-up time interactions are to be helpful, then teacher training progammes need to prepare teachers for interactions with parents and why the end of the day is preferable for parents. In addition, teachers need to be skilled in communication as well as child development.

Furthermore, teachers' schedules ought to allow for end-of-the-day interactions with parents. For instance, the end-of-the-day shift might end a half an hour after the childcare centre closes so that teachers could talk with parents and have time to straighten up their classrooms after families have left. Moreover, teachers could be offered overtime to meet with parents after hours. Childcare centres need to recognize that the end of the day is parents' preferred time to talk with teachers and that many teachers believe it is important to talk with parents as soon as a problem arises and that waiting to talk during a scheduled conference is counterproductive.

(Kennedy Reedy and Hobbins McGrath, 2008: 354–5)

Points to Ponder

- Would Abbey and Julia (in the story) agree with the researchers' suggested solutions? Why do you think this?
- Is time for discussion a big issue in an early childhood setting that you know? If so, how has this happened?

Points to Discuss

- Do you think that early childhood education and care staff believe that their primary role is to educate and care for children and that communicating with parents is only a secondary role?
- Do you believe that staff schedules could be changed to include Damien's hope (in the story) for '15 minutes at the end of the session'? How could this work? Who would pay for it?

Research Snippet 2: Parents as partners in early childhood services in Ireland: an exploratory study (Martin, 2003)

Martin (2003) used non-participant observations and self-report questionnaires to study how staff and parents saw their relationships with each other. The participants were 79 parents in Dublin using full-time care for their children and the 48 staff in 34 services providing that care.

Some key findings

- Most parents wanted to participate more in the early childhood programme, but felt constrained by a lack of time.
- Many parents felt that staff did not have the time to build partnerships with parents.
- Traditional (and pervasive) models of parent involvement used in these services assumed that parents could be involved in the setting during the day, so a new **model** was needed that included parents who work during the day.

Points to Ponder

- Do you think that the lack of time for conversations with staff affects all parents equally, or can some parents make better use of snatches of time than others?
- Why do you think that staff in the study assumed that parents could be involved in their children's education and care during the day? Is this assumption common in the research about parent involvement (or the lack of it)?

Points to Discuss

- Are you happy with the way that early childhood education and care settings organize time? How could they improve?
- When there is insufficient time for good staff–parent communication and relationships, who is disadvantaged?

Fairness Alert

Time becomes a political issue when it is a scarce resource whose distribution is inequitable in its effects. For example, a parent who shares a teacher's cultural and linguistic background may be able to use scarce time more efficiently than a parent from a different background. As we have seen in the story and in the research, early childhood education and care settings often give staff and parents insufficient time to communicate effectively and this is a particular instance of an unfair thinking habit called 'silencing' – making it difficult for an individual or a group to be seen and/ or heard. Busy pick-up and drop-off times with minimal staffing can silence parents' questions, interests and concerns, despite staff goodwill. In this particular situation we focus on silencing voices through how time is organized.

- Staff can silence parents and vice versa when lack of time makes it difficult for them to communicate effectively with each other.

Here is an example of silencing from the story:

Shayna: It's always sort of rushed . . . when you get here it's rushed and when you're leaving, um, you can sort of sense that the staff are tired and there is too much going on. You encourage us to talk to you at any point if we've got queries, but lots of times I've waited until it's my time, but you're sort of at the tail end and the kids are running out there. . . .

Here is an example of silencing from the research into staff–parent relationships:

At times when many children are being dropped off and picked up at the same time, the communication – at best – is reduced to the mere necessities. I can feel disappointed when I come to pick him up in the evening. You don't even find out if . . . he can't even tell us . . . what he has done. No, they don't know. Did he eat well? Well, they don't know that either because they weren't the ones there during the morning hours. (Sandberg and Vuorinen, 2008: 155)

Why silencing is unfair

- Practices as well as words can silence views and perspectives when they do not invite alternative ideas or views to be expressed.
- Communication that is one-way (e.g. 'telling' or 'informing') implies that other people's views are not wanted and/or irrelevant.
- It assumes/implies that there is a hierarchy of knowledge, with professional knowledge at the top.
- It relies on and reinforces professionals defining the hierarchy of knowledge, preventing other types of knowledge from reaching the top.
- It implies that professionals produce knowledge and that non-professionals' role is merely to be grateful.

How you can counter silencing

- Try to increase and improve the opportunities for parents' questions, ideas and views to be heard at pick-up and drop-off times.
- Assume that parents from all ethnic, cultural and language groups have valuable ideas and views about their children's education that could help staff.
- Actively encourage individuals and groups to express their ideas and views about young children's education and care and welcome them as valid.

- Actively create circumstances where holders of 'non-mainstream' views about young children feel comfortable expressing them because their ideas are treated with respect. Do not assume that you have succeeded in doing so – always ask.
- Be prepared to rethink your ideas about young children's education and care if they fail to reflect the experiences of families with whom you work.
- Try to use 'different from', rather than 'better than' when comparing and contrasting different sources and types of knowledge about young children.
- If you encounter ideas and practices that you find unacceptable, explain your position, rather than just assert it as a professional . . . and be prepared to rethink your position if circumstances change.

Points to Ponder

- Do you think that the parents at Treetops (in the story) feel silenced by the lack of time?
- How did time 'silence' parents in the centre where Abbey (in the story) worked previously? Could she have done anything to change that?
- Should staff find extra time to communicate effectively with parents? Do you agree with *Aretha* (in the story) that 'it doesn't seem fair that they have to do this'?

Points to Discuss

- Have you been silenced by the way in which an organization structured time? If it happens again, could you behave differently?
- In your experience, are people from particular gender, class, ethnic or cultural groups more likely to be silenced by the way in which early childhood education and care settings structure time?

Models of staff–parent relationships around time

'The organization of time' might seem an abstraction, but the story and the research show that it can have very real effects on communication and relationships between parents and staff. Below are two models of staff–parent relationships around time. Model 1 appears in two articles advising staff about their relationships with parents: one about how to reduce stress for working parents (Whiren, 1992); the other about using classroom rituals and traditions to build a sense of community (Scully and Howell, 2008). Model 2 emerges from our own research with parents and staff in Australia (MacNaughton, 2004). The models are followed by some 'Points to Ponder' and some 'Points to Discuss', which may help you decide what you think about the significance of time to staff–parent relationships.

> ### Model 1: Time-related problems can be solved through goodwill and some extra effort

First of all, assign a staff member to be available at the point of entry. She can greet *both* parent and child, give or receive information relevant to caregiving, and support the parent and the child during separation. Occasionally she may need to assist with the removal of wraps. Parents may be under special time constraints if weather is bad, they've arrived at the center late, or traffic snarled.

Remember that the parents are on their way someplace else. They need to be reassured about the child and then to be able to leave for work. (Whiren, 1992: 35)

Monthly family breakfasts are another tradition in the class; one that began when some parents suggested morning as a convenient time to visit the classroom. On the first Friday of each month, parents bring a breakfast food to share and spend some time getting to know the other children and parents in a relaxed and informal setting. Parents stay as long as they are able and some even linger through the first circle. (Scully and Howell, 2008: 263)

> ### Model 2: Time-related problems have effects that are inequitable

'Scarce' time may work best for parents who share a teacher's cultural and linguistic background. So is time and its distribution fundamentally linked to questions of respect for social, cultural and linguistic diversity? Can we respect social, cultural and linguistic diversity without paying attention to questions of time and its distribution? And can we do this without work intensification for staff? Time is a political issue when it is a scarce resource whose distribution is inequitable in its effects. To see these effects, staff, parents and policy makers need to reflect on how they distribute time and who is silenced and who is heard through 'snatched time' with parents and the boundaries it creates. (MacNaughton, 2004: 5)

Points to Ponder

- Which model of staff-parent relationships around time is closer to yours?
- How do you think that *Aretha* and Julia (in the story) would each respond to the sorts of suggestions for increasing time with parents that constitute Model 1?

Points to Discuss

- In your experience, who does well and who does badly when time is a scarce resource in early childhood education and care settings? What sorts of people in the story are being disadvantaged by the scarcity of time?
- Why do you think that time is a scarce resource so often in early childhood education and care settings?

Further reading to deepen your thinking and talking

Hedge, A. and Cassidy, D. (2004) Working with families: teacher and parent perspectives on looping. *Early Childhood Education Journal*, 32(2): 133–8.

Hedge and Cassidy (2004) examined parent and teacher perspectives on the introduction of what they call 'looping' in a childcare setting. Looping involves an adult carer staying with a group of children over time, rather than children moving onto new adults each year. Looping enables parents and staff to build relationships over several years and, therefore, may enable them to deal with having only 'scarce time' to talk on any given day.

Monna, B. and Guathier, A. (2008) A review of the literature on the social and economic determinants of parental time. *Journal of Family Economic Issues*, 29: 634–53.

In their literature review, Monna and Guathier (2008) found that the amount of time parents spend with their children depends on the parent's social and economic background. However, they also found that parents who work and parents who do not differed very little in how long they spent with their children, because parents who work tend to give up their sleep and leisure activities (e.g. watching television) rather than give up time with their children. So, for example, each hour a mother is in paid work reduces the time spent with her children by only three minutes a day.

References

Hedge, A. and Cassidy, D. (2004) Working with families: teacher and parent perspectives on looping. *Early Childhood Education Journal*, 32(2): 133–8.

Kennedy Reedy, C. and Hobbins Mcgrath, W. (2008) Can you hear me now? Staff-parent communication in child care centres. *Early Child Development and Care*, 180(3): 347–57.

MacNaughton, G. (2004) Children, staff and parents: building respectful relationships in New Zealand and Australian early childhood contexts – the Australian context. *Australian Journal of Early Childhood*, 29(1): 1–7.

Martin, S. (2003) *Parents as Partners in Early Childhood Services in Ireland: An Exploratory Study*. Dublin: Dublin Institute of Technology.

Monna, B. and Guathier, A. (2008) A review of the literature on the social and economic determinants of parental time. *Journal of Family Economic Issues*, 29: 634–53.

Sandberg, A. and Vuorinen, T. (2008) Preschool–home cooperation in change. *International Journal of Early Years Education*, 16(2): 151–61.

Scully, P. and Howell, J. (2008) Using rituals and traditions to create classroom community for children, teachers, and parents. *Early Childhood Education Journal*, 36(3): 261–6.

Whiren, A. (1992) Reducing stress for working parents. *Day Care and Early Education*, 9(26): 26, 35.

2 Understanding the professional

To help you quickly grasp who's who, practitioners' names are shown in upright font and parents' names are shown in *italic* font.

Davina is in the final year of her early childhood degree course and has just started her final **practicum** at Windy Peak Children's Centre. On her second day at Windy Peak, a child – David – in Davina's room wanted a bike that another child was riding and Davina said that he had to wait his turn. David started screaming, Davina repeated quietly what she had said and walked away. Just then, David's father – *Roger* – walked in, pointed to his son and shouted at Davina, 'Why don't you do something about the boy? You can see he's upset – do something!' Davina started to explain that it is important not to reinforce a child's negative behaviour as it encourages the child to repeat this behaviour, but *Roger* ignored her and attended to his son. The next day, in her lunch break, Davina talked to two of the Centre's trained staff – Helen and Pam – about the incident.

Davina: I tried to tell him that I was doing it because we don't want to reinforce negative behaviour, but he just ignored me. What should I have done?

Helen: Oh, you don't want to pay any attention to Roger. He's OK, really, but he's always going off like that.

Pam: But it's not just Roger, is it? Lots of the parents think that all we do is play with their kids all day and that we don't know any more about their kids than they do. We need to get across to the parents that what we do with the kids is based on observations and theory and stuff. We're not just playing with them.

Helen: When Jenny did a round-table discussion with a group of parents, it was really interesting to see the light going on. You know, it finally dawned on them – 'Oh my God, all those observations and records and that – this is why they do them!' Once Jenny explained to them how we actually use our observations and our training and all that, and why we do things like we do, it was good.

Pam: Every now and then, you'll get a parent who says, 'What have you been doing today?' But we put that in our newsletters – you know, what the program is about, that sort of thing.

Davina: So why don't parents read the newsletters?

Helen: I think they do – well, some of them do. But I don't think something written is ever as effective as actually communicating verbally with parents. Every one of us could read the same thing and get something totally different out of it. I think you really need to talk it out to be clear about it.

Davina: So just because it's in writing, that doesn't mean that the parents will necessarily get it?

Helen: I suppose the best you can hope for is that parents will understand that we do what we do because we're professional and qualified.

Pam: I think sometimes we feel self-conscious if the parents are around for too long, you know? So we can give the impression that we don't want them around, even though we know we ought to want them around, and sometimes we actually kind of enjoy having them around. . . . There should be nothing to hide, but you would just be . . . very self-conscious and not confident the parents will read the situation like we do.

Davina: That's when I find it hard, when parents are around . . . because then I feel I have to explain what I'm doing all the time.

Helen: That's right, if they're there I'll usually say something like, 'Oh, he's doing that because . . .', I don't know, '. . . because he's at that developmental stage', or something, you know.

Pam: You just explain to them, because they do look uncomfortable or they'll go over to their child and (pause) it does happen. I mean, I know that's my first reaction when parents come in and it feels almost guilty to keep explaining why you are doing something, but . . .

Helen: But it makes sense to them if you explain to them. (Pause) Sometimes.

Resources for thinking and talking about staff–parent relationships

Research Snippets

Researchers are documenting the changing nature of staff–parent relationships in early childhood education and care and especially how staff use their formal, professional knowledge. Research Snippet 1 (Addi-Raccah and Arviv-Elyashiv, 2008) examines the tensions in Israeli schools between parents' increasing involvement and teachers' view of themselves as professionals. It raises issues very similar to those raised by Davina, Helen and Pam (in the story) about having parents in their classrooms.

Research Snippet 2 is from two research projects that explored the impacts of professional knowledge on communication between staff and parents (Elliott, 2003; Lasky, 2000). In contrast to Helen's hope in the story that 'parents will understand that we do what we do because we're professional and qualified', the projects found that parents regarded most of what the staff told them as irrelevant to what they wanted to know!

Following each Research Snippet are some 'Points to Ponder' and some 'Points to Discuss', which may help you decide what you think about Helen's, Davina's and Pam's attitudes to their status as professionals.

> ### Research Snippet 1: Parent empowerment and teacher professionalism: teachers' perspectives (Addi-Raccah and Arviv-Elyashiv, 2008)

Addi-Raccah and Arviv-Elyashiv (2008) asked Israeli teachers how they regarded parents' involvement and especially what they thought about the power relations between teachers and parents. The participants were 12 'home room' teachers in schools for children between six and twelve years old.

Some key findings

Most teachers were worried about parents' increasing power and control over how teachers did their job. For example:

> Parents have many opportunities to come to school and say things and criticize everything. They are allowed to do whatever they want . . . they have a lot of power. Whatever they want, they get. . . . It is an invasion of our privacy. Parents come to school and criticize our work. They can do whatever they want. (Shirley).
> (Addi-Raccah and Arviv-Elyashiv, 2008: 402)

> The boundaries have become blurred. Once parents are at the school, school is the parent. . . . Parents are not afraid. They have no inhibitions. The school is theirs. We serve them. (Beth).
> (Addi-Raccah and Arviv-Elyashiv, 2008: 402)

When parents are dissatisfied with a teacher, they organize, and together they protest and complain. Together they are very strong. (Ann).   (Addi-Raccah and Arviv-Elyashiv, 2008: 403)

Teachers in my school express their concern about parents' attitudes and behavior. Some of them perceive parents' greater involvement as threatening. (Liz).

(Addi-Raccah and Arviv-Elyashiv, 2008: 404)

Points to Ponder

- What tensions around professional knowledge and qualifications were revealed in parent–teacher relationships? In the story, did Davina, Pam and Helen experience similar tensions to those in this Research Snippet?
- How did the teachers regard themselves: as experts (in teaching), as collaborators (with parents), as partners (with parents) or as uncertain of their role?

Points to Discuss

- Can staff work effectively if parents do not understand why they act as they do with the children?
- Do you know any early childhood education and care staff who, like Pam, feel 'self-conscious if the parents are around for too long'? Why do they feel this way?
- Do you know any parents whom early childhood staff might call 'threatening', as Liz the Israeli teacher described parents in her school?

Research Snippet 2: Sharing care and education: parents' perspectives (Elliott, 2003) and The cultural and emotional politics of teacher–parent interactions (Lasky, 2000)

The quotes in this snippet are from two studies. The first two quotes are from a study (Elliott, 2003) of Australian parents' views on their relationships with early childhood staff. Researchers interviewed 36 parents from 13 early childhood services in culturally and socially diverse areas of western Sydney in five separate focus groups. The final quote is from a study (Lasky, 2000) of 53 Canadian primary and secondary teachers' views about their relationships with parents.

Some key findings

- In Elliot's (2003) study, parents believed that there was discontinuity between children's experiences in the services and at home; and that much of what staff told them was uninteresting. For example:

  Information evenings and orientation sessions should answer parents' questions not simply tell us (parents) what they (staff) want us to know.   (Elliott, 2003: 16)

  Look, I don't know if I'm expecting too much to ask them to explain the education they're providing to my child to me, but I really am interested to know, but I don't know how to ask and they don't offer me the information.   (Elliott, 2003: 17)

- Lasky (2000) found that teachers dominated communication with parents, who often felt uncertain about how to ask questions they wanted answered. For example:

  . . . parent communication during student conferences was bound by silent rules of discourse. They likened it to discourse between doctors and patients. The teacher was in control, choosing the topics of discussion, dominating the interaction and talking about students from their perspective. Bernhard (1999) found that a combination of fear and a cultural tendency to defer to the authority of teachers often prevented parents from asking clarifying questions.   (Lasky, 2000)

Points to Ponder

- What did each study reveal about parents' and staff's expectations of 'good communication'? Why do you think their expectations differed?
- Do these research findings add anything to Davina's realization that 'just because it's in writing, that doesn't mean that the parents will necessarily get it'?

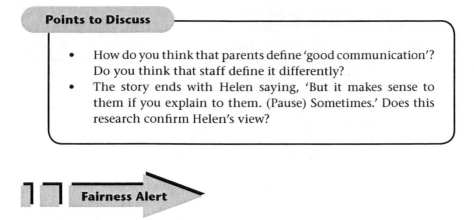

Points to Discuss

- How do you think that parents define 'good communication'? Do you think that staff define it differently?
- The story ends with Helen saying, 'But it makes sense to them if you explain to them. (Pause) Sometimes.' Does this research confirm Helen's view?

Fairness Alert

The story and the research literature on staff–parent relationships include some examples of an unfair thinking habit called 'privileging' – giving more weight to one set of views or experiences over any others. In this specific instance, we focus on privileging one form of knowledge over another.

- Privileging staff's formal, professional knowledge about children in general over parents' informal, anecdotal knowledge about their specific children.

Here is an example of privileging from the story:

Helen: I suppose the best you can hope for is that parents will understand that we do what we do because we're professional and qualified.

Here is an example of privileging from the research about parent involvement:

A teacher stated, 'I have no problem with parents participating in my curriculum decisions as long as I make the final decision. Parents can give their opinion but they may not determine what I do'.
(Addi-Raccah and Arviv-Elyashiv, 2008)

Why privileging is unfair

- It implies that parents' views are always less significant than staff views, no matter who the parents and staff are.
- It assumes and reinforces the idea that there is a hierarchy of knowledge, in which the sort of professional and scientific knowledge that staff possess is always at the top.

How you can counter privileging

- Assume that parents and early childhood education and care staff have a right to be respected for their particular knowledge of children.
- Do not assume that 'good' parents should defer to staff's 'greater knowledge'.
- Regard differences in opinions (e.g. about educating and caring for children) between staff and between staff and parents as normal and desirable.
- If you are a staff member, explain to parents why you act with children as you do, ensure that they understand you and then invite them to ask you any questions. Actively encourage parents to tell you if they disagree with how you are educating and caring for their children and show that you value their replies.
- If you are a parent, ask staff why they act with children as they do, especially if they behave differently to you. Ensure that you understand their answers and tell them if you do not.
- If you are a student, look for and document occasions when staff and parents showed themselves open to different sorts of knowledge about children's care and education.

Points to Ponder

- Do you consider yourself an expert in the education and care of young children?
- Have you heard teachers' expert knowledge privileged in discussions about young children's curriculum?

Points to Discuss

- What have been the main sources of your knowledge about children?
- Who do you think should have the final say about young children's curriculum?

Models of staff–parent relationships around knowledge

People think in different ways about the relationship between professional knowledge and parents' knowledge. For example, Davina, Pam and Helen (in the story) were confident that they possessed professional knowledge about young children, yet uneasy when parents saw them putting that knowledge into practice.

Below are two contrasting models of relationships around knowledge of young children between families and early childhood staff. Model 1 appears in Lasky's (2000) study of 53 Canadian primary and secondary teachers' views about their relationships with parents and in Niemeyer's (2001) review of research about how to include families of children with disabilities in early childhood teachers' training (Niemeyer, 2001). Model 2 underpins an article about the use of indigenous knowledge in early childhood development policies and practices (Pence and Schafer, 2006). The models are followed by some 'Points to Ponder' and some 'Points to Discuss', which may help you decide what you think about the attitudes to teachers' professional knowledge and to parents' anecdotal knowledge expressed by the characters in the story.

Model 1: An early childhood curriculum should express teachers' professional knowledge

---

Parents think they are experts in education and it amazes me. I had a student come back after I had marked their paper. There was a very nasty note, written by the parent, that it was the most outrageous marking they had ever seen, and what were my criteria, etc., etc.

(Lasky, 2000: 856)

I sent a message home through his son. I said, 'You can come and see me, no problem, but I'm much too busy to write a written report.' I told him he was not qualified to comment on what I was doing. And I said, 'What would you think if I presumed to walk into your office and tell you how to do your job, and yet you think you can comment on my job. You're not qualified. Good, you're concerned about your kid, but don't think you're going to intimidate me into giving him more marks, because, you're not.' They have such naive expectations.

(Lasky, 2000: 856)

If the disciplines of the university administrators (department chair, dean or provost) are different from early childhood or child development, these university administrators may not understand or support the importance of involving families in teacher training activities. Consequently, they may be resistive in providing contractual agreements with family members who do not have a college degree or any experience in the area of **special education** or child development. Or they may consider a programme that involves family members in training as less rigorous or lacking in quality. (Niemeyer, 2001: 178)

> **Model 2: An early childhood curriculum should include parents' knowledge about their children**

Anne Gamurorwa's project similarly focused on traditional stories, using story-telling "competitions" judged by local audiences. This approach proved highly successful and adjacent districts requested support in creating similar events. (Pence & Schafer, 2006: 7)

Gamurorwa found in her research that the culture of storytelling has been dwindling in Uganda with the rise of urbanization and the shift from extended to nuclear family living arrangements, modern cultural influences, the demands of formal education, and family struggles for economic survival. Her work aimed not only to document existing storytelling, therefore, but also to revive interest among the current generation of parents, caregivers and children, creating, "awareness among parents and caregivers about the rich indigenous knowledge that can be tapped in promoting holistic development of children, morally, spiritually, intellectually and emotionally".
(Gamurorwa, 2004: 5 [cited in Pence & Schafer, 2006: 7])

After receiving approval from story-tellers, Gamurorwa developed learning modules for preschool programmes based on the stories provided, which then became part of training seminars she conducted for **preschool** instructors. (Pence and Schafer, 2006: 7)

Points to Ponder

- Which model of staff-parent relationships around knowledge is closer to yours?
- Do you think that Pam's self-consciousness around parents (in the story) would exist if parents had featured in her professional training?
- Can you think of any story-tellers who could feature in the professional development of early childhood education and care staff?

Points to Discuss

- What are your models of staff-parent relationships around knowledge? How do they resemble each other? How do they differ?
- If you are a staff member or a student, how does your model influence your work with young children?
- If you are a parent, how does your model influence your relationships with the staff who educate and care for your child/ren?

Further reading to deepen your understanding

Pence, A. and Schafer, J. (2006) Indigenous knowledge and early childhood development in Africa: the early childhood development virtual university. *Journal for Education in International Development*, 2(3): 1–16.

We used parts of this article in Model 1, but reading it in full also shows how 'Western' knowledge of child development has been privileged over indigenous knowledge of young children in diverse contexts. The authors describe a project in Uganda that challenged such privileging and they discuss how to challenge such privileging of one type of knowledge over another.

Wilgus, G. (2005) 'If you carry him around all the time at home, he expects one of us to carry him around all day here and there are only two of us!', Parents', Teachers' and Administrators' Beliefs about the Parent's Role in the Infant/Toddler Center.' *Journal of Early Childhood Teacher Education*, 26: 259–73.

Wilgus (2005) is a good introduction to privileging . . . and to othering, and homogenizing! In her study of a public day care programme in New York, Wilgus found a range of models of staff-parent relationships around knowledge. One end of the range was the belief that staff should tell parents how to raise their children; the other end was the belief that staff have no right to tell parents how to raise their children! As usual in such studies, the really interesting models are in the middle of the range.

References

Addi-Raccah, A. and Arviv-Elyashiv, R. (2008) Parent empowerment and teacher professionalism: teachers' perspectives. *Urban Education*, 43(2): 394–416.

Elliott, R. (2003) Sharing care and education: parents' perspectives. *Australian Journal of Early Childhood*, 28(4): 14–21.

Lasky, S. (2000) The cultural and emotional politics of teacher-parent interactions. *Teaching and Teacher Education*, 16(8): 843–60.

Niemeyer, J. (2001) Involving families in training early childhood educators: developing a framework for family centeredness. *Journal of Early Childhood Teacher Education*, 22(3): 173–9.

Pence, A. and Schafer, J. (2006) Indigenous knowledge and early childhood development in Africa: the early childhood development virtual university. *Journal for Education in International Development*, 2(3): 1–16.

Wilgus, G. (2005) 'If you carry him around all the time at home, he expects one of us to carry him around all day here and there are only two of us!' Parents', Teachers' and Administrators' Beliefs about the Parent's Role in the Infant/Toddler Center.' *Journal of Early Childhood Teacher Education*, 26(3): 259–73.

3 Revealing ignorance

To help you quickly grasp who's who, practitioners' names are shown in upright font and parents' names are shown in *italic* font.

As in many early childhood centres, staff and parents at Corryong Street Children's Centre have found it hard to create and sustain positive relationships with each other. About three years ago, the staff group decided that the key to good relationships with parents is to admit that staff do not know everything about young children. Each year, the centre sets aside a half-day when staff and parents review its philosophy and curriculum. We join them as Kieran – the Director – is moving the discussion to staff–parent communication. *Erin* and *Fran* are parents; Judy, Maeve and Joan are staff members.

Kieran: OK, let's move on to talk about communication between parents and staff. We decided some time ago that good communication between parents and staff means building shared understandings about children; and to build those shared understandings, each side has to actually listen to what the other side says. We also decided that parents will feel more confident to say what they really feel about their children's time here if staff admit to them that they don't have all the answers about children. So the question is – how are we going?

Erin: I can't speak for all the parents, of course, but I think that some of us feel now that we can trust the Centre more because the staff here regard our ideas and beliefs about our children as valid and important. They don't just dismiss us because we're 'over-reacting' or 'insecure' or something, or that we don't actually know what we're talking about!

Fran: That's right. Some parents are starting to feel more comfortable because you lot don't just tell us what you know about our kids. You also tell us when you're unsure about something and that no-one has all the answers, which makes it easier for us to tell you about things we're not sure of. And that's not just about the children. People on both sides now say when we're not sure about the different cultures represented here and when you say that, people can see that you're interested in what they do and you learn more about their values and so on.

Judy: I've been here almost a year now and I must admit that when I first came across all this 'admit your ignorance' stuff, I thought it was a bit weird! I mean, I didn't spend three years at college so I could say to parents, 'Oh, don't ask me – I don't know'! I'm still not sure about it, but I have to admit, parents here seem more confident about saying what they think than in other Centres I've worked in. I don't know if that's the ignorance thing . . . but it's something.

Maeve: Well, I think it definitely helps when you say that you don't know everything. I think that parents are then definitely more comfortable when we say that we're going to talk about what *we see* as being true, and that we're going to talk about issues that may be difficult to talk about. Like at the moment in our room, there is a lot of aggression, but I think parents aren't seeing us as 'the experts' who know it all, who they've got to compete with. I think they're opening up and feeling more comfortable saying, 'We don't know what to do about it'. And I feel more comfortable saying, 'Well, I don't know the answer', you know, and 'Have you got any ideas?' I think it makes for a more honest relationship.

Joan: Well, I've found that when parents can see that they can really affect what I'm doing, it helps me because it makes me question how I operate and what I do. And I think that helps open up spaces for people on the fringe, who are silenced. It gives them more of a voice, somehow.

Judy: Of course, admitting your ignorance is never easy and it always has consequences. If we really take on board what parents say, it means that we're not always going to be right. If we really are talking about parents having a real voice, then we have to start asking 'Who are we?' Are we the experts who always know what's best for children and their parents? Because if we aren't, we have to think about deferring to parents sometimes. And that can be hard for professionals to do.

Erin: Yes, everyone has to say 'There are no right answers – there's only lots of possibilities'. And as a parent, you just want to do what's right for your child.

Kieran: Having said all that – and I suppose I'm summing-up here – let's be clear that there has to be a bottom line at some stage. We take everyone's ideas on board, we try to understand where everyone's coming from, in terms of their beliefs. You try not to force the issue, but if you have to – because of a safety issue, say – then you draw the line.

Joan: But I think there'd still be on-going discussions with families afterwards about it, wouldn't there?

Resources for thinking and talking about staff–parent relationships

Research Snippets

There is not much research featuring early childhood staff who admit they are uncertain! From that small amount of research, here are two Research Snippets, each chosen because its findings are relevant to the issue of uncertainty in professionalism raised in the story. Research Snippet 1 is taken from Secrest McClow and Wilson Gillespie (1998), which describes how staff and parents in a USA **Head Start** programme learnt together about an approach to teaching and learning that was new to them. The findings reflect Erin's statement in the story that 'some (parents) feel now that we can trust the Centre more because the staff here regard our ideas and beliefs about our children as valid and important.' Research Snippet 2 comes from a review by Knopf and Swick (2008) of research on staff–parent relationships and it shows how staff and parents can use focus groups to explore issues of common concern.

Following each Research Snippet are some 'Points to Ponder' and some 'Points to Discuss', which may help you decide what you think about the role of professional uncertainty in the relationships between the staff and parents at Corryong Street.

Research Snippet 1: Parental reactions to the introduction of the Reggio Emilia Approach in Head Start classrooms (Secrest McClow and Wilson Gillespie, 1998)

When a Head Start programme in the USA introduced the **Reggio Emilia** approach to teaching and learning for the first time, Secrest McClow and Wilson Gillespie (1998) used focus group interviews to study the reactions of parents of children in the programme.

Some key findings

- Parents and teachers were uncertain about what a Reggio Emilia approach to teaching and learning involved.
- Parents were concerned about the new approach and suggested ways to improve communication about the new approach between staff and parents. Specifically, the researchers found that:

The key to easing the minds of the parents seems to lie in communication, through providing them with resources to educate them on the Reggio Emilia approach. We feel that when staff provide parents with more educational information about what the children are doing in the classroom, parents will feel much more comfortable about the Reggio Emilia approach.

(Secrest McClow and Wilson Gillespie, 1998: 134)

Focus groups where both teachers and parents were present proved to be important in fostering communication between the parents and staff. One teacher expressed her concern that she is still familiarizing herself with the Reggio Emilia approach and feels a bit inept in conveying the information to parents. She feels she does not know the information as well as she would like to. Parents in this group provided support to the teachers, and suggested they could learn together.

(Secrest McClow and Wilson Gillespie, 1998: 134)

Points to Ponder

- Do you think that the staff member who said that she felt 'a bit inept' was being professional or unprofessional?
- Do you think that Judy (in the story) would find it easy to admit to feeling 'a bit inept'?

Points to Discuss

- What do you think would happen in an education and care setting you are familiar with if a staff member said to parents that they felt 'a bit inept'?
- To what extent does Research Snippet 1 support Kieran's approach to working with parents?

Research Snippet 2: Using our understanding of families to strengthen family involvement (Knopf and Swick, 2008)

Knopf and Swick (2008) reviewed the current research literature (primarily from the USA) on staff–parent relationships to suggest effective strategies to improve staff–parent communication in early childhood settings.

Some key findings

- Effective strategies include home visits, surveys and questionnaires, focus groups, telephone calls, emails, parent conferences and family communication journals.
- Of particular relevance to the issues raised in the story is the use of staff–parent focus groups:

A particular strategy to educate all early childhood professionals is the focus group (Swick 2003). The focus group strategy offers a unique opportunity to gain the parental perspective. If placed within a trusting and supportive context, focus groups help parents articulate their views on issues and concerns related to their children's education and our involvement in that process. One example comes from a student in the author's family dynamics class. After participating in a one hour parents' group discussion that focused on teacher–parent relations she was amazed that the basic concerns of parents were being sure their child was safe at school, received fair treatment, was challenged to grow and learn, and to hear from the teacher on a regular basis. This student noted: "I would never have thought how basic the concerns of the parents would be and the teacher who was directing the focus group said the same thing." Indeed, focus groups can empower everyone because they give us new lenses to see how we interact with parents and families.

(Knopf and Swick, 2008: 426)

Points to Ponder

- In an early childhood education and care setting you know, what communication strategies promote communication between parents and staff most effectively? Do these strategies enable staff and parents to learn from each other?
- What do you think are the pros and cons of using focus groups of parents and staff?

Points to Discuss

- Would you welcome 'new lenses' through which to see parent–staff relationships? Why (or why not)?
- Would you feel comfortable in a focus group of staff and parents? Which staff members from Corryong Street Children's Centre (in the story) would you like to have in the focus group? Why?

Fairness Alert

The story and the research literature on staff–parent relationships include some examples of an unfair thinking habit called 'silencing' – making it difficult for an individual or a group to be seen and/or heard. Specifically, in this case we focus on how knowledge can be used to silence.

- Silencing parents by invoking professional knowledge and expertise.

Here is an example of silencing from the story:

> Joan: Well, I've found that when parents can see that they can really affect what I'm doing, it helps me because it makes me question how I operate and what I do. And I think that helps open up spaces for people on the fringe, who are silenced. It gives them more of a voice, somehow.

Our example of silencing from the research is from a project in which early childhood students in the USA set up an Infant Toddler Information Fair for Parents as part of their initial teacher training course (Freeman and Knopf, 2007). The following quote we use explains why the course leaders took this decision:

> We believed it (An Infant Toddler Information Fair for Parents) offers students a valuable opportunity to begin speaking with a professional voice and to interact with parents as interested and informed professionals. The assignment (Appendix A) required students to work collaboratively in groups of three to five to develop a tri-fold display and family-friendly handout focusing on a particular developmental

domain or a developmental task typically mastered during the birth–36 month period. . . . Displays and handouts were shared with an authentic audience of parents and caregivers at a late afternoon Parent Information Fair at our on-campus lab site. Representative topics included developing and supporting healthy attachments, age-typical fears, making friends, large motor development, and fine motor skills.   (Freeman and Knopf, 2007: 143)

Why silencing is unfair

- It assumes/implies that people 'on the fringe' should defer to professionals and learn from them, while professionals can learn nothing from 'non-professionals'. (For example, in the research, staff created An Infant Toddler Information Fair for Parents – why was there no equivalent Fair for staff, created by parents?)
- It assumes/implies that professionals' role is to transmit knowledge to 'non-professionals', whose role is merely to be grateful. (For example, the students produced 'a family-friendly handout' *for* parents and caregivers, not *with* them.)

How you can be fair

- Actively seek ideas and views about young children's education and care that are outside the mainstream.
- Actively create circumstances where holders of 'non-mainstream' views about young children feel comfortable expressing them and where their ideas are treated with respect. Do not assume that you have succeeded in doing so – always ask.
- If you are an early childhood education and care staff member or student, be prepared to rethink your ideas about young children's education and care if they fail to reflect the experiences of families with whom you work.
- If you are an early childhood education and care staff member or student and you encounter ideas and practices that you find unacceptable, explain your position, rather than just assert it as a professional . . . and be prepared to rethink your position if circumstances change.
- If you are a parent who feels silenced, ask other parents if they feel the same and, as a group, ask staff for explanations, not assertions.

Points to Ponder

- How did parents in the story challenge silencing? How did staff react?
- Have you experienced people from a particular gender, class, ethnicity or cultural group being 'silenced' by professional knowledge?
- How do you think that *Erin* in the story would react to an Infant/Toddler Parent Information Fair?

Points to Discuss

- Have you ever been 'silenced' because of your (alleged) ignorance? (Perhaps it happened outside of an early childhood context.) If so, what was similar and different about your experiences? Why was this?
- Have you have seen someone rely on their professional knowledge (and status) to make things happen? If it happened to *Fran* in the story, how do you think that she would react?

Models of professional knowledge in staff–parent relationships

There are several different ways to think about the role and power of professional knowledge in staff–parent relationships. In the story, parents *Erin* and *Fran* are clear that it can silence parents, but staff member Judy is proud of her professional knowledge and uncertain whether setting it aside is necessarily a good idea.

Below are two models of the place of professional knowledge in staff–parent relationships, each one illustrating current debates about what characterizes an early childhood education and care professional. In both models, professional knowledge is never final, but always provisional and open to question. This resembles Maeve's and Joan's position (in the story) – all they can do is to state their perspective on early childhood matters and see what other perspectives emerge.

Model 1 has its foundations in three sources: research by Kuisma and Sandberg (2008) about Swedish students' and preschool teachers' views of professionalism; a literature review by Souto-Manning and Swick (2006) about how teachers see parent involvement; and a critical reflection by an early childhood teacher (Barnes, 2005) on uncertainty in professional knowledge. Model 2 underpins a study (Doucet, 2008) of how African-American parents in the USA prepared their children for transition – either from preschool to kindergarten or from kindergarten to first grade.

The models are followed by some 'Points to Ponder' and some 'Points to Discuss', which may help you decide what you think about the different attitudes to uncertainty expressed by the characters in the story – and whether you would like to be a parent, teacher or student at Corryong Street Children's Centre.

Model 1: Professional knowledge is messy and uncertain, learnt and unlearnt

---

Preschool teachers can develop these reflective discussions in situations consisting of 'uncertainty, instability, uniqueness, and value conflict' (25). Other concepts that influence development in professionalism are teachers' thinking and reframing. When teachers become conscious of their own frames, according to Lidholt (1999), they also become conscious about alternative ways of framing practical situations. Reflections have led to change and renewal in work. To be able to use reflection for this purpose, preschool teachers need a basis in the form of theories, perspectives and knowledge in several fields, in the organization, in content, in discussions and in social relationships in preschools.

(Kuisma and Sandberg, 2008: 194)

Recently I read Ebbeck's (2003) argument that poststructuralism is useless to teachers if its critique does not tell them how to act. I suggest that Ebbeck's argument can only be valid if we accept that teaching is simply a technical task, and that in undertaking this task, teachers can *know* how to act. My experiences tell me the opposite – that teaching is unknowable, complex, contextual, unpredictable, contradictory, messy and intensely personal. (Barnes, 2005: 15)

A lifelong learning approach in which the teacher learns alongside children and families: We made ourselves vulnerable and envisioned our roles as symbiotically teaching and learning alongside our students and their families. We kidwatched (Owocki and Goodman, 2002) and based our teaching on the observations we made regarding how children learn, their interests and sociocultural backgrounds. We constantly sought to embody a posture that conveyed our deep value and respect for parents' funds of knowledge (Moll and Greenberg, 1990). Finally, we let children and parents see us in learning roles, not only by participating in community events and going to professional conferences, but by learning from them and valuing their backgrounds, histories, and interests in developing curriculum and classroom settings that were embracing of diversity.

(Souto-Manning and Swick, 2006: 191)

Model 2: Professionals' race and culture can limit or enhance what they know

---

Another facet of teaching children about culture and race for these parents and carers was sharing information about their ancestry as African-Americans, exemplifying the *Black cultural experience perspective*. Charles (MC father) said this:

One of the things we did as a family was we sat down and we watched 'Roots' together. . . . And we had discussion afterwards. And the reason I felt that that was important was because I want them to understand the importance of education. What people had to go through so that they could even have a school or a quality school to learn, so that it wouldn't be taken for granted . . . I think it's important especially for African-Americans to know their history so that they can appreciate it and not take it for granted.

In Peters's (1985) study of racial socialization among middle-class and working-class parents of toddlers, several themes parallel to the ones in the current study also emerged: "Teaching children to survive", "The importance of self-respect and pride", "Understanding that fair play may not be reciprocal", "A good education: a top priority", and "But most of all – love".

What stands out from the findings of the current study when compared with others is the consistency of ideas expressed by Black parents, who recognize that race and racism will be issues in their children's lives as it is and has been in their own lives, although they may choose to emphasize different issues when teaching their children about culture and race.   (Doucet, 2008: 127)

Points to Ponder

- Which model of uncertainty in relationships between parents and staff is closer to your view of these relationships?
- If you are a parent, do you think that uncertainty can help staff in an early childhood education and care setting to develop their professional knowledge?
- If you are a staff member, do you agree with Maeve's view (in the story) that, 'Well, I think it definitely helps when you say that you don't know everything.'?

Points to Discuss

- How does your own racial and ethnic background and experience affect what you feel certain about and what you don't? Could this influence what you need to learn about?
- Do you think that early childhood staff should learn how to admit uncertainty as part of their training? If so, how should they regard the rest of their training?

Further reading to deepen your understanding

Souto-Manning, M. and Swick, K. (2006) Teachers' beliefs about parent and family involvement: rethinking our family involvement paradigm. *Early Childhood Education Journal*, 34(2): 187–93.

Souto-Manning and Swick (2006) present the key beliefs and practices of what they term a 'traditional paradigm' of parental involvement and then call for a research-based rethink of it. They urge staff to remain curious about children and to learn with and from parents; and they encourage staff to ensure that their chosen theories of children, learning and education reflect children's culturally and ethnically diverse experiences and understandings.

Urban, M. (2008) Dealing with uncertainty: challenges and possibilities for the early childhood profession. *European Early Childhood Education Research Journal*, 16(2): 135–52.

Urban (2008) poses a new form of professionalism in early childhood that 'embraces openness and uncertainty, and encourages co-construction of professional knowledges and practices. Research, in this frame of thinking, is understood as a dialogic activity of asking critical questions and creating understandings across differences, rather than producing evidence to direct practice' (p. 135). His new form of professionalism challenges early childhood professionals and policy-makers to rethink how professionals acquire and use professional knowledge.

References

Barnes, S. (2005) Unsettling and resettling pedagogical knowledges, in G. MacNaughton (ed.) *Doing Foucault in Early Childhood Studies*. Oxford: Routledge: 13–16.

Doucet, F. (2008) How African American parents understand their and teachers' roles in children's schooling and what this means for preparing preservice teachers. *Journal of Early Childhood Teacher Education*, 29(2): 108–39.

Freeman, N. and Knopf, H. (2007) Learning to speak with a professional voice: initiating preservice teachers into being a resource for parents. *Journal of Early Childhood Teacher Education*, 28(2): 141–52.

Knopf, H. and Swick, K. (2008) Using our understanding of families to strengthen family involvement. *Early Childhood Education Journal*, 35(5): 419–27.

Kuisma, M. and Sandberg, A. (2008) Preschool teachers' and student preschool teachers' thoughts about professionalism in Sweden. *European Early Childhood Education Research Journal*, 16(2): 186–95.

Secrest McClow, C. and Wilson Gillespie, C. (1998) Parental reactions to the introduction of the Reggio Emilia approach in Head Start classrooms. *Early Childhood Education Journal*, 26(2): 131–6.

Souto-Manning, M. and Swick, K. (2006) Teachers' beliefs about parent and family involvement: rethinking our family involvement paradigm. *Early Childhood Education Journal*, 34(2): 187–93.

Urban, M. (2008) Dealing with uncertainty: challenges and possibilities for the early childhood profession. *European Early Childhood Education Research Journal*, 16(2): 135–52.

4   Joining in – the benefits and costs

To help you quickly grasp who's who, practitioners' names are shown in upright font and parents' names are shown in *italic* font.

The Sunrise Kindergarten believes very strongly in involving the children's parents in their work. Julie is a teacher at Sunrise and today she is attending a half-day professional development workshop on 'Building Better Parent Involvement'.

Fiona: Welcome, everybody. My name is Fiona and I will be your facilitator for today's workshop on building better parent involvement. Now, as we all know, parent involvement benefits the children, it benefits the staff and, of course, it can be very beneficial to the parents themselves. When parents join-in, it shows that their relationships with the staff are good and the research tells us that this is a good thing for the children. I don't think I'm saying anything controversial here, am I?

Marg: No. When parents join in, it's a wonderful support to staff. It makes your job so much easier. It's like an extra pair of hands in the room.

Karly: That's right. When parents join-in, it makes you feel that they care about what you're doing and want to come in and be involved and be supportive. Like, we put a sign up, you know, we need some new dolls clothes, or dress-ups or something, and it was, 'Oh, I can sew. What would you like?' And they can see that we're thrilled with the clothes and the children are using them. And we love it, because it's something that we just don't have time to do ourselves.

Fiona: OK. So when parents join-in, it can mean an extra pair of hands in the room and extra resources for the children. Are there any other benefits?

Olive: If the parents are involved, they can tell other parents about what we're doing. We've often had a parent come to the centre and say, 'Oh, do you remember so-and-so? They talked about their child's experience here. They loved being here.' And that's word of mouth. If the parents can't join-in what goes on, then they can't actually convey that to other people. (Murmurs of agreement.)

Julie: I always try to encourage parents to contribute any special experiences or resources that they may have. So, for example, if a parent does an unusual job or if they've just been somewhere unusual, I ask them to come in and tell the children about it. Or if they can do something special, like play a musical instrument, I ask them to do that. It adds to the experiences I can give the children.

Marg: And parents are really good at just giving some of their time, whether it's helping out in the classroom or doing a bit of maintenance in the building, those little jobs that we can't do because time's so tight.

Fiona: This all sounds marvellous! Everything's just fine! (Laughter) Why are we here today, then? It's all been sorted out!

Renee: Well, one problem I've had is parents coming in who have very strong personal philosophies about a particular issue. And when they're involved, this can be difficult. A child may do something, like hit another child over the head with a block and parents can react very differently. We'd probably step in and say, 'That's a block. What do you use that for? That's right – to build with. Now look at so and so. You really hurt them. Let's *build* with the blocks.' (Laughter) Whereas a parent will say, 'Don't you hit him over the head with that! That's naughty!' (More laughter)

Fiona: So parents can react strongly sometimes to things that they don't like?

Marg: Absolutely! There's some parents it's better not to encourage too much.

Renee: That doesn't mean the opportunity isn't there and we'll support them, but there are some parents that I wouldn't encourage as much as some others who I can see have beautiful gifts to share with the children.

Marg: But you've got to be consistent with the children. You can't say one thing to them and have a parent say something different, because you'll just confuse them.

Karly: And look, we are meant to be professionals and to use our professional knowledge . . . that most parents don't have. So we have to set some boundaries.

Fiona: So are you saying, then, that you like parents to become involved, provided that you can set boundaries around it?

Renee: Well yes, I think we are . . . aren't we?

Resources for thinking and talking about staff–parent relationships

Research Snippets

Here are two snippets from the research concerning parents' participation in early childhood education and care programmes. Research Snippet 1 is from a study by Bers et al. (2004) in Argentina, which examined what happened when parents, staff and four- and five-year-old children collaborated to build a robot, blurring the boundaries of status between them. Research Snippet 2 comes from a study in which Kuisma and Sandberg (2008) asked early childhood staff whether their status as professionals affected their relationships with parents.

Following each Research Snippet are some 'Points to Ponder' and some 'Points to Discuss', which may help you decide what you think about the issues Renee, Marg, Karly and Fiona raise about parents joining in their programme.

Research Snippet 1: Teaching and learning when no one is expert: children and parents explore technology (Bers et al., 2004)

Bers et al. (2004) studied a technology project in Argentina in which parents, teachers and children collaborated to build a robot. The participants were 10 families from a range of cultural and religious backgrounds (Jewish, Christian, Muslim, Indian-American, European, Chinese, and Caucasian) who had four- and five-year-old children, together with the children's early childhood teachers. The researchers used informal observations, interviews (including pre-project interviews), reflections and photographs.

Some key findings

- As teachers observed parents and children collaborating, they discovered what parents knew about their children's learning.
- Parents' involvement made parents' knowledge and expertise more visible to teachers:

    The notion that parents represent valuable sources of support and information regarding children's learning experiences and potentials is not widely recognized by educators (New, Mallory, and Mantovani, 2000). And yet the pride and pleasure taken by parents who had such firsthand experiences with their own children – and the potential uses of the knowledge gained – was fully visible to the teachers of the children in the study.

Different families had different working styles, and parents had varying expectations of what should be happening. It was not always easy for all of the parent-child dyads to become comfortable with each other as they shared new roles as both teachers and learners. Unanticipated was the finding that, in most of the cases, the parents, not the children, had the most difficulties adjusting to this shifting status from expert to novice.   (Bers et al., 2004)

Points to Ponder

- Do you think that the participants' different backgrounds influenced the outcomes of the technology project?
- Which staff members (in the story) would enjoy being involved in the technology project and which ones would not?

Points to Discuss with another adult

- In an early childhood education and care setting you know, do parents 'join in' on their terms or on the staff's terms? (Be honest!)
- To what extent do you agree with Marg's statement (in the story): 'There's some parents it's better not to encourage too much.' Do you think that Marg might change her view if she was involved in a project like the one described by Bers et al. (2004)?

Research Snippet 2: Preschool teachers' and student preschool teachers' thoughts about professionalism in Sweden (Kuisma and Sandberg, 2008)

Kuisma and Sandberg (2008) explored the attitudes of preschool teachers and student preschool teachers towards being an early childhood professional, a day care attendant and a 'recreational pedagogue'. The participants were 27 Swedish preschool teachers and 30 student teachers attending a Swedish university; and they completed written questionnaires about their views on professionalism.

Some key findings

- Participants believed that professionalism is associated with knowledge, ability and experience. They defined 'ability' as either 'scientific' knowledge gained through studying for a professional qualification, or as experience gained through practical activities with children, colleagues and parents and through co-operation with social services in the community.
- Participants emphasized that knowledge changes with time, that teachers could never become skilled enough and that post-qualification training developed the core of their professional knowledge. The teachers also believed that professionalism developed through discussion forums where pedagogical questions arose, through the pedagogical network and through action research in groups of children. Therefore, to develop professionally, a teacher had to want to learn new things:

Professionalism develops through an interplay between education, reflection and further training. It keeps pedagogical awareness alive. (Teacher)   (Kuisma and Sandberg, 2008: 190)

Points to Ponder

- How did the participants believe that professionalism is related to knowledge and to experience?
- Do you think that parents with 'very strong personal philosophies about particular issues' (Renee, in the story) would find it easy to be involved in the sort of project that Kuisma and Sandberg (2008) described?

> **Points to Discuss**
>
> - For staff members or students: how did each of you acquire your professional knowledge? What are the strengths and weaknesses of 'professional' knowledge?
> - For parents: Do you think that reacting 'strongly sometimes to things that they don't like' (Fiona, in the story) can keep teachers on their toes as professionals?

Fairness Alert

In the story, Renee, Marg and Karly each felt that not all parents who 'join in' have the appropriate knowledge and skills to help staff. Their views are examples of an unfair thinking habit called 'privileging' – giving more weight to one set of views or experiences over any others. Specifically, in this example we highlight privileging one form of knowledge over another, its effects and how it might be countered.

- Privileging staff's professional expertise concerning children in general over parents' knowledge and opinions concerning their specific children.

Here is an example of privileging from the story:

> Renee: Well, one problem I've had is parents coming in who have very strong personal philosophies about a particular issue. And when they're involved, this can be difficult. A child may do something, like hit another child over the head with a block and parents can react very differently. We'd probably step in and say, 'That's a block. What do you use that for? That's right – to build with. Now look at so and so. You really hurt them. Let's build with the blocks.' (Laughter) Whereas a parent will say, 'Don't you hit him over the head with that! That's naughty!' (More laughter)

Here is an example of privileging from the research into staff–parent relationships:

Other teachers may simply regard themselves as the expert and do not acknowledge the importance of specific familial knowledge of a particular child (Hilliard and Pelo, 2001; Hurt, 2000; Keyser, 2001). Such attitudes act as shields that impede parent participation. In order to encourage parent participation, teachers have to truly believe that the parents have valid and worthy opinions (Gonzalez-Mena, 1999). Beyond this, teachers must invite and welcome such opinions. Jones et al. (1997) conducted a study which focused on variables affecting teacher attitude towards parental involvement. Results of this study indicate that teachers' attitudes are affected by the ability level of the students and by the teachers' race but are not affected by grade level taught, or teachers' degree of experience and education.   (Carlisle et al., 2005: 158)

Why privileging is unfair

- It dismisses parents' knowledge about their particular children as less important that staff's knowledge about children in general.
- It assumes that staff's views on children's learning will – by definition – always be more valuable than parents' views.
- It assumes that professionals will always have 'the right answer'. This ignores the fact that professional knowledge changes over time, so 'the right answer' can be different at different times.

How you can counter privileging

- Assume that parents and staff have equal rights to express their ideas about how best to educate and care for children.
- Regard parents' knowledge and professionals' knowledge as supplementing each other, not competing against each other.
- If you are a staff member or a student, look for opportunities to develop your knowledge by learning from parents.
- If you are a parent, share what you know about your child/ren with other parents, to find similarities to, and differences from staff's professional knowledge.

Points to Ponder

- If you are a student, do you think that your training is privileging professional expertise over other sorts of knowledge? Do you think that this matters?
- Do you believe that each parent has 'beautiful gifts to share with the children' (Renee, in the story)? If you are a parent, what is your 'beautiful gift'?

Points to Discuss

- Do early childhood staff need to discover what parents know about their children in order to do their work properly?
- Should early childhood staff defer to parents as experts in regard to their children?

Models of parent–staff relationships around professional expertise

The story and the research show that for staff, inviting parents to 'join in' is far from a jolly affirmation that 'we're all in this together'! Instead, it is fraught with ambivalence and ambiguity. For example, Renee valued parents' 'beautiful gifts to share with children', but Karly thought that as a professional, she should set boundaries around what parents can and can't be allowed to do.

Below are two quite different models of professional expertise. Model 1 emerges from the review by Carlisle et al. (2005) of research (mainly from the USA) about influences on parents' involvement in their children's education. The review shows clearly that a high percentage of teachers believe that many parents cannot be involved effectively in classrooms because they lack the appropriate knowledge. Model 2 comes from a study in Germany by Griebel and Niesel (2009), which presents parents as valuable partners to staff in planning for children's learning. The models are followed by some 'Points to Ponder' and some 'Points to Discuss', which may help you decide what you think about the different attitudes to professional expertise expressed by the characters in the story.

Model 1: Parents do not necessarily know how best to help their children's learning

Ninety per cent of teachers responding to a survey on parental and family involvement agreed that parental involvement is vital to having a good school; however, 73% disagreed with the statement that "most parents know how to help their children" (Jones et al., 1997: 160). These responses indicate that teachers view parents as less than competent when it comes to helping children with schoolwork. The issue, however, may simply indicate a discrepancy in what is expected by parents and teachers. Research by Aaroe and Nelson (2000) indicates that "parents, especially those who are culturally diverse, tend to have a lack of knowledge regarding the behavioral standards expected in the schools" (p. 321). This lack of knowledge can be and often is detrimental to those parents who then volunteer in their child's classroom without the knowledge of what is considered proper behavior for either themselves or the students. Teachers' expectations for both students and parents must be attainable and must be made clear.   (Carlisle et al., 2005: 158)

Model 2: Parents' knowledge about their children is essential to planning children's learning

Although both families and educators have legitimate roles and responsibilities, the emphasis is not on the roles families can play for schools. Rather the emphasis is on relationships, specifically on finding ways for families and educators to work together to promote the academic and social development of children. Improved collaboration between kindergarten staff and primary school teachers requires knowledge about the contents and methods of each other's work as well as working conditions. They also need a shared understanding of the child as a learner and as an individual coping with transition to school. As for parents, educational partnership requires an understanding of the developmental demands on mothers and fathers whose first child becomes a school pupil. On the professionals' part, knowledge about the situation and needs of parents could be improved, and greater efforts made to interact with parents as partners in promoting children's educational success.

> Parents are always involved in education, either as silent, passive partners or as vocal, active partners. Traditional approaches to family involvement which emphasize involving parents in ways that address the school's agenda, prescribing traditional roles for parents such as volunteering or homework helper, have been successful for children of middle-class families where there is continuity between the needs, beliefs and knowledge about education of school and families.
>
> (Griebel and Niesel, 2009: 64)

Points to Ponder

- Which model of the role of expertise in early education programmes is closer to yours?
- Do you think that the best way for parents to be involved in young children's education is to 'contribute special experiences or resources' (Julie, in the story)?

Points to Discuss

- Do you believe that people who work with young children require professional knowledge about them?
- Do you agree with Marg's statement in the story, 'But you've got to be consistent with the children. You can't say one thing to them and have a parent say something different, because you'll just confuse them.'?

Further reading to deepen your understanding

Amirali Hamida, J. and Henley Walters, L. (2008) Including parents in evaluation of a child development program: relevance of parental involvement. *Early Childhood Research and Practice*, 10(1), Expanded Academic ASAP. Available online at www.uiuc.edu/v10n1/jinnah.html (accessed 7 June 2010).

Amirali Hamida and Henley Walters (2008) examined the pros and cons of including parents' views when evaluating an early childhood programme and offered ways to understand the value of parents' knowledge in early childhood programmes. They compared and contrasted the links between a parent's level of involvement in the programme and their evaluation of that programme. Do you think that reading this article would change Renee's view (in the story) that only parents with 'beautiful gifts to share with the children' should be encouraged to be involved?

Osgood, J. (2006) Professionalism and performativity: the feminist challenge facing early years practitioners. *Early Years*, 26(2) 187–9.

Osgood (2006) examined several different approaches to professionalism in early childhood education and care. She argued that a feminist approach to professionalism emphasizes co-operation and critical reflection on diverse sources of information and knowledge. Could those qualities improve knowledge relations between staff and parents? How do you think Osgood would approach the exchange between Karly and Fiona (in the story) about setting boundaries around parent involvement?

References

Amirali Hamida, J. and Henley Walters, L. (2008) Including parents in evaluation of a child development program: relevance of parental involvement. *Early Childhood Research & Practice*, 10(1): Expanded Academic ASAP. Available online at www.ecrp.uiuc.edu/v10n1/jinnah.html (accessed 7 June 2010).

Bers, M., New, R. and Boudreau, L. (2004) Teaching and learning when no one is expert: children and parents explore technology. *Early Childhood Research & Practice*, 6(2): Expanded Academic ASAP. Available online at www.ecrp.uiuc.edu/v6n2/bers.html (accessed 2 June 2010).

Carlisle, E., Stanley, L. and Kemple, K. (2005) Opening doors: understanding school and family influences on family involvement. *Early Childhood Education Journal*, 33(3): 155–62.

Griebel, W. and Niesel, R. (2009) A developmental psychology perspective in Germany: co-construction of transitions between family and education system by the child, parents and pedagogues. *Early Years*, 29(1): 59–68.

Kuisma, M. and Sandberg, A. (2008) Preschool teachers' and student preschool teachers' thoughts about professionalism in Sweden. *European Early Childhood Education Research Journal*, 16(2): 186–95.

Osgood, J. (2006) Professionalism and performativity: the feminist challenge facing early years practitioners. *Early Years*, 26(2): 187–9.

5 We speak English here

To help you quickly grasp who's who, practitioners' names are shown in upright font and parents' names are shown in *italic* font.

Carol is attending a job interview at the Blackbush Childcare Centre in suburban Melbourne. She is Anglo-Australian and has worked in long day care for 20 years. She has no formal early childhood qualifications, but has just started a Diploma in Early Childhood course at the local college. Here is a short excerpt from the job interview, followed by an excerpt from the panel's discussion afterwards.

Bree: Welcome, Carol. Come in and sit down. My name's Bree and I'm the Children's Services Co-ordinator from the local Council. This is Sally, the Centre's Co-ordinator and this is *Aisah*, whose daughter Adik comes to this Centre.

Sally: Carol, as you know, early childhood staff are working increasingly with diverse ethnic and cultural groups. Blackbush is a good example. Several of our families speak several languages and we have a very inclusive approach to working with them. What would you see as your priorities when you are working with children whose home language isn't English?

Carol: Well, I think it's important for all children to learn English. If they can't speak English, they are at a real disadvantage living here, because Australia is an English-speaking country.

Aisah: And so would you encourage children to speak in their home language?

Carol: Well, I think that's best done at home, because the parents will know what to do, won't they? When the child's here, I'll teach them English, because if they don't speak English, they won't be able to communicate with other people. And if they do speak English, they can translate between us and their parents. Parents who don't speak English generally come from cultures that don't see education as we do, so they don't get involved. But if their children start to speak English, this might help the parents to participate more in the centre.

The post-interview discussion

Aisah: Adik is very confident in speaking and communicating to our family and friends in Malay Bahasa. That is our first language and I really want her to know and feel confident and comfortable in using this language. I feel very worried that Carol would not support this and would always encourage her to use English. I don't want Adik to learn that English is the only language that Australians should speak.

Bree: I agree with *Aisah*. We need to get better in Australia at using and respecting all the languages that people speak here. After all, there were over 500 indigenous languages spoken here before English become the dominant language, before people came to think that being Australian means speaking English.

Sally: I don't know. It's very hard. We can't expect the staff to speak every language spoken in Australia. I come from a Greek-Australian background, but I only speak English. But I think I can still talk to each of the parents equally.

Bree: Look, I'm Anglo-Australian, but if we only speak English aren't we saying that English is best? Are we really treating people equally if they have to speak as we do, just because we think it's best?

Sally: But let's be honest – in any society, one group will dominate it and so its language becomes 'the norm'. My Greek dad learnt the hard way – the only way to be an Australian is to speak English. (Pauses) Mind you, my parents have been living here for 40 years and they still get asked where they're from!

Aisah: Australia is a very diverse society, yet lots of people think that English is 'the norm' and a mark of Australian citizenship. But I don't think you have to speak English to be Australian. My parents don't speak English but they are Australian citizens. I wonder how Carol would communicate with them?

Sally: Carol's very experienced. I am sure she would know what to do. I suspect that your parents will begin to learn English once they mix with us here at the Centre, *Aisah*. Won't that be terrific?

Aisah: (Quietly) I'm not sure that they'd want to come here. (Looks away)

Resources for thinking and talking about staff–parent relationships

Research Snippets

Here are two snippets from the research about first and second languages. Research Snippet 1 is from a study of mock 'child conferences' between preschool teachers and adult students of English posing as parents (Hooks, 2008). The aim was to prepare the preschool teachers to communicate more effectively with non-English-speaking children and parents. This is a very different approach to Carol's and Sally's view (in the story) that 'English is best'.

Research Snippet 2 is from a complex study in which Jewish and Palestinian parents discussed their decision to send their children to bilingual primary schools in Israel (Bekerman and Tatar, 2009). While it concerns parents with children in primary schools, those parents' particular attitudes to language reflect some of the attitudes expressed in the story. In particular, Research Snippet 2 reveals attitudes to bilingualism (Jewish parents wanted to 'do the right thing'; Palestinian parents wanted their children to succeed) that Bree and Sally expressed in the story.

Following each Research Snippet are some 'Points to Ponder' and some 'Points to Discuss', which may help you decide what you think about the place of languages in early childhood education and care settings – and whether you would employ Carol (in the story).

Research Snippet 1: Help! They don't speak English: partnering preservice teachers with adult English Language Learners (Hooks, 2008)

Hooks (2008) documents an experiment in the USA in which 44 preservice teachers held mock 'child conferences' with adult English Language Learners posing as parents. The aim was to increase preservice teachers' ability to communicate more effectively with non-English-speaking children and parents and Hooks interviewed the preservice teachers before and after their mock 'child conferences'.

Some key findings

- Pre-'conference':
  - 95.5 per cent of the preservice teachers were nervous, especially because of the issue of language. Few had had significant prior contact with people with limited English.
- Post-'conference':
  - 48 per cent of the preservice teachers said that the conference increased their ability to communicate with parents in general, not just with parents with English as a second language (e.g. preparation, putting parents at ease, eye contact, starting on a positive note, building rapport).
  - 43 per cent of the preservice teachers said that the conference increased their confidence to work with parents for whom English is a second language.
  - 41 per cent of the preservice teachers said that the conference broadened their awareness and understanding of diversity. For example:

This experience helped me see that diversity is not just limited to black and white and Hispanic, but includes a variety of ethnicities and cultures. Just when I think that I am thinking 'diversity', something else comes along to open my eyes a little wider. Most importantly, all cultures are valuable and worth exploring.

(Hooks, 2008: 102)

Points to Ponder

- Why do you think that so few of the preservice teachers had had significant prior contact with people with limited English? Does this reflect your own experience?
- In your experience, does early childhood teachers' training prepare them sufficiently to work in culturally diverse communities? Would Carol (in the story) agree?

Points to Discuss

- Researchers have shown consistently over many years that language is a problem in early childhood settings. Why do you think that this problem is so persistent? How do you think that *Aisah* (in the story) would answer the question?
- Is an early childhood teacher's primary task to educate and care for children, with communicating with parents coming second? Or are the two equally important? How is this issue addressed in the story?

Research Snippet 2: Parental choice of schools and parents' perceptions of multicultural and co-existence education: the case of the Israeli Palestinian-Jewish bilingual primary schools (Bekerman and Tatar, 2009)

Bekerman and Tatar (2009) undertook a complex study of parents' choice of school in Israel, in which Jewish and Palestinian parents discussed their decision to send their children to bilingual primary schools. The participants were six Palestinian and six Jewish parents from two bilingual schools. They had participated in an earlier study, which had shown them to be involved in their children's primary school and to support its aims.

Some key findings

- Palestinian parents saw competence in Hebrew as crucial to their children's academic development, but feared that their children would be assimilated; Jewish parents feared that their children bore the consequences of their parents' 'ideological' choice of school.
- For Palestinian parents:

  The schools offer their children a buffered opportunity to meet the majority group and also one which will help them adopt psychological dispositions (not necessarily supported by their cultural background) considered of great importance for their future functioning in a modern society.

  (Bekerman and Tatar, 2009: 180)

For example:

> This school challenges the kids. The have to learn the other. And I can say even the enemy, okay? You have to learn to live with the enemy. (Bekerman and Tatar, 2009: 180)

> (B)etter than separate schools. Because . . . when you see the other, you know yourself better. . . . When you see only yourself, when you look in the mirror you see only your face. And you can't compare your face with other faces.
> (Bekerman and Tatar, 2009: 181)

- Jewish parents liked the school's welcoming atmosphere and were less concerned with bilingualism and national identity. For example:

> We are part of the hegemonic community here in Israel, it's there, it's like Hebrew being the dominant language in the school. . . . So I don't feel threatened and I don't need to strengthen my identity.
> (Bekerman and Tatar, 2009: 181)

- Palestinian parents saw the schools as one more opportunity to get to know the 'other', supporting present and future social interactions; the schools made Jewish parents realise that the Palestine-Israel conflict cannot be resolved easily:

> I spoke with this Arab colleague and I realized that there are narratives that can't be reconciled, it's not just a question of finding the truth which we'll never do.
> (Bekerman and Tatar, 2009: 181)

Points to Ponder

- Do you think that the Palestinian parents' desire for their children to learn Hebrew contradicted their desire to promote Palestinian national identity? How did *Aisah* (in the story) deal with this issue?
- If a parent asked you to recommend a bilingual school, which two languages would feature in the school you recommended? How did you come to this conclusion?

> **Points to Discuss**
>
> - Which two languages does each of you think should be taught at a bilingual school in a community featuring a diversity of languages? How did you come to this conclusion?
> - Do you think that describing a language as 'other than English' makes it sound secondary or subordinate to English? How do you think that Bree (in the story) would answer this question?

Fairness Alert

The story and the research literature on staff–parent relationships include some examples of an unfair thinking habit called 'homogenizing' – assuming that everyone in a particular group (e.g. a gender, a class, an ethnicity or a culture) is the same. This ignores the perfectly normal and usual differences between people within a group. Specifically, in this case we examine how staff and parents can homogenize each other's actions and perspectives.

- Staff can homogenize parents and vice versa – 'Oh, they're all like that!'
- Staff can homogenize parents from diverse backgrounds whom they think are uninvolved in their children's education.

Here is an example of homogenizing from the story:

Carol: Parents who don't speak English generally come from cultures that don't see education as we do, so they don't get involved. But if their children start to speak English, this might help the parents to participate more in the centre.

Here is an example of homogenizing from the research literature. It comes from a qualitative USA study of English Language Learners being taught by 44 preservice teachers majoring in early childhood studies (Hooks, 2008). The following quote is from one of those preschool teachers who is explaining what she learnt from her teaching experience with English Language Learners.

I also learned that because someone speaks another language does not mean that they do not have the same feelings as you do. The student (of English) I spoke with, her friend and her herself, as mothers, they cared for their children just as much as an English speaking parent cares for their child.   (Hooks, 2008: 103)

Why homogenizing is unfair

- People from any culture are complex individuals. Despite their shared cultural background, their experiences of education will not necessarily be the same.
- People within a particular culture (including you) will have had different experiences of education.
- Researchers may find broad trends (e.g. attitudes to education) in a culture, but not every individual in that culture will conform to those broad trends.

How you can counter homogenizing

- Assume that people from different cultures may have had different experiences and that this may affect their attitudes to education.
- Be prepared to learn about the specific ways in which each family sees its children's education.
- Look for statements or actions that homogenize a group of people (e.g. a culture, a racial group) and challenge them.

Points to Ponder

- Can you make general statements about the members of a group without homogenizing them? Did the characters in the story homogenize 'Australians'?
- If everyone is an individual, can we make any general statements about people? (If you are a student, or a staff member contemplating some professional development, these questions are especially pertinent.)

Points to Discuss

- Can you think of positive ways to homogenize the members of a group?
- In your experience, what sorts of people are homogenized – 'They're all like that'?

Models of staff–parent relationships around language and culture

Clearly, when language policy becomes entangled with homogenizing, many diverse points of view can come into play! Carol and Sally (in the story) had no real problems with the dominance of English, while Bree and Aisah each had considerable concerns about it. Below are two very different models of the place of language in relationships between staff and parents. Model 1 is from a study of how teachers in a British multiethnic primary school saw the involvement of and interest of parents from Pakastani backgrounds in their children's language and literacy learning (Huss-Keeler, 1997). Model 2 is from the study by Bekerman and Tatar (2009) introduced above. (A reminder: it is a study of Israeli and Palestinian parents' perspectives on their choice to send their children to bilingual primary school.)

The models are followed by some 'Points to Ponder' and some 'Points to Discuss', which may help you decide what you think about the different attitudes to languages in early childhood settings expressed by the characters in the story.

Model 1: Non-English-speaking parents are uninvolved in their children's education because they regard it as the school's responsibility

A lot of them (Pakistani parents) have the attitude that the education of their children is not their responsibility. It's the responsibility of the school and the school should get on with it. . . . A lot of it is the language barrier. They can't understand what we're saying, but I also think they don't think it's their place to know what we're saying and what we're doing. They don't think it's for them to do. School is for school to do and home is for home to do. . . . (A) lot of these parents won't have been to school or have been to a foreign school.

(Huss-Keeler, 1997: 175)

Model 2: Parent involvement programmes can reproduce existing cultural inequalities

de-Carvalho (2001) . . . critically claimed that parental involvement is often presented as a policy 'solution' for low achievement and inequality in the educational system, especially in the US and in other Western countries. Although parental involvement is proposed as a means to enhance or even equalize school outcomes, the ideal involvement projects still fit and empower the upper-middle class families and do not 'invite' culturally and social-class diverse and powerless families into the educational settings.

(Bekerman and Tatar, 2009: 182)

Points to Ponder

- Model 1 criticizes parents for their non-involvement, while Model 2 criticizes parent involvement programmes for reproducing inequalities. Which model is closer to your view of parent involvement programmes? Was inequality an issue for the characters in the story?
- In the absence of a translator, (how) could you establish rapport with someone who does not speak your language?

Points to Discuss

- In your experience, what sorts of parents generally get involved with their children's education? Which do not?
- Do you think that parent involvement programmes – however good – can effectively counter the effects of social and economic disadvantage on young children's educational achievement?

Further reading to deepen your understanding

Kenner, C. (2005) Bilingual families as literacy eco-systems. *Early Years*, 25(3): 283–98.

Kenner (2005) argues that young children in bilingual families become proficient in languages not through the 'story reading with parents' approach generally prescribed by schools, but in different ways with different family members. The term 'literacy ecosystems' both captures that diversity of approaches and highlights that some languages are 'endangered species'. The article's emphasis on families' diverse literacy practices/teaching is a good counterpoint to essentialist dismissals of non-English-speaking families as uninterested in their children's education.

Fred Ramirez, A. (2003) Dismay and disappointment: parental involvement of Latino immigrant parents. *Urban Review*, 35(2): 93–108.

Fred Ramirez (2003) interviewed Latino immigrant parents in California (USA) about their views and experiences of parent involvement in their child's school. The findings showed that parents were keen to be involved in their children's education but faced many barriers.

References

Bekerman, Z. and Tatar, M. (2009) Parental choice of schools and parents' perceptions of multicultural and co-existence education: the case of the Israeli Palestinian-Jewish bilingual primary schools. *European Early Childhood Education Research Journal*, 17(2): 171–85.

Fred Ramirez, A. (2003) Dismay and disappointment: parental involvement of Latino immigrant parents. *Urban Review*, 35(2): 93–108.

Hooks, L. (2008) Help! They don't speak English: partnering preservice teachers with adult English Language Learners. *Journal of Early Childhood Teacher Education*, 29(2): 97–107.

Huss-Keeler, R. (1997) Teacher perception of ethnic and linguistic minority parental involvement and its relationships to children's language and literacy learning: a case study. *Teaching and Teacher Education*, 13(2): 171–82.

Kenner, C. (2005) Bilingual families as literacy eco-systems. *Early Years*, 25(3): 283–98.

6   We respect 'their' culture

The story

To help you quickly grasp who's who, practitioners' names are shown in upright font and parents' names are shown in *italic* font.

The Daybreak Childcare Centre is in an area with a predominantly Anglo-Australian population and Min is a four-year-old Chinese-Australian child who will start attending the Centre soon. Min has just moved with her mum and dad to Melbourne from Ballarat, where each generation of the family has lived since the 1860s. (Min's great-great-grandfather came to Australia during the 1860s gold rush.) Jo is the co-ordinator of Daybreak and she is discussing how Daybreak can support Min and her family with Tanya and Trish, who work in the room where Min will be. All three staff are Anglo-Australian.

Jo: It's quite late in the year and I am aware that children have already formed quite strong friendship groups. How are you planning to make Min feel welcome in your room?

Tanya: Well, I thought we might have a Chinese theme in the room for the first week or so. That might be a good way to show Min and her family that we respect their culture.

Trish: Yes, that would be fun. Maybe we could have some Chinese food so she has something that is familiar to her?

Jo: Do you know what her favourite foods are? I think her mother said she really likes pasta.

Trish: How funny, that's not really part of her culture is it? She's lucky to have a culture with such great food. I really like Chinese food.

Tanya: It will be good to do some cultural things with Min. We don't really do many cultural things. I might learn some Chinese songs and I think I saw a story about a Chinese girl with a duck or something – 'Ping' I think it was called – at the back of the cupboard.

Trish: We probably could go to the Resource Centre for some cultural-type stuff. I think that it's important that Min and her family see that we respect their culture.

Jo: Yes, I suppose lots of our resources are very much about our culture.

Trish: What do you mean, *our* culture?

Jo: Well, all of us on the staff here are all Anglo-Australians so we tend to use songs and stories that we know or that we feel comfortable to us. That's what I meant by 'our culture'.

Trish: You see . . . I don't think of my self as '*Anglo*-Australian' . . . just as . . . Australian. I'm not sure what my culture is . . . (Pauses) . . . It's just normal Australian culture, I suppose.

Tanya: I wonder what would happen if we asked the parents how they see their culture here? I wonder what they'd say?

Trish: But then, what's 'culture' anyway? What's it mean? Are you *in* a culture? Do you *have* a culture? Obviously, Min's Chinese, but is that her culture? I don't know.

Resources for thinking and talking about staff–parent relationships

Research Snippets

Here are two snippets from the research concerning cultural diversity and early childhood education and care. Research Snippet 1 is from a study of early childhood education and care programmes on a Native American Indian reservation in Montana, USA, in which parents' involvement was at the heart of a developing, culturally sensitive curriculum (Gilliard and Moore, 2007). Research Snippet 2 is from a broad-ranging survey of the research on the place of 'race' and ethnicity in parent involvement programmes in schools in the UK (Crozier, 2001). Following each Research Snippet are some 'Points to Ponder' and some 'Points to Discuss', which may help you decide what you think about how Jo, Tanya and Trish (in the story) each try to respect 'other' cultures and what 'normal' Australian culture is.

Research Snippet 1: An investigation of how culture shapes curriculum in early care and education programs on a Native American Indian reservation (Gilliard and Moore, 2007)

Gilliard and Moore (2007) studied how culture shapes curriculum in three early childhood education and care programmes in a Native American Indian reservation in Montana, USA. There were eight female **early childhood**

educators with at least three years experience as participants and seven of those eight were Native American Indians. The researchers wrote reflective journals, field notes and engaged with participants via questionnaire-guided interviews.

Some key findings

The literature suggests that the largely European American teaching force is unprepared to work with an increasing population of ethnically diverse children (Banks, 2002; Nieto, 2002). Thus educators fail to link home and community culture to school culture, failing to foster a sense of belongingness in children that promotes academic achievement (Moore, 2004a; Osterman, 2000).

(Gilliard & Moore, 2007: 257)

- Participants saw their work with children and parents as influenced less by 'culture' and more by respect and understanding; and saw their roles as 'honoring and perpetuating the day-to-day rituals, routines and beliefs of the place in which they lived. . . . "The parents' personal wishes, beliefs and ideas about child care are honoured and respected in the classroom." (Gilliard and Moore, 2007: 254–5)
- Several rituals brought together children, parents, teachers and the broader community; and ritual drumming was associated with daily classroom activities.
- All the educators involved parents – even extended family – in their programmes, sought parents' beliefs and values and used them to transform their curriculum. For example, one educator invited parents to vote on elements of her programme and activities; another invited parents to bring their tribal language into her programme through, for example, word labels and music.

The teachers did not describe parents' wishes as frustrating or inconvenient as is often case with educators who offer a fixed or static curriculum (Goldstein, 2003; Moore with Seeger, 2005); but, rather, they welcomed family input and saw the care and education of the children in their programmes as a partnership between themselves and parents.

(Gilliard and Moore, 2007: 257)

Points to Ponder

- Do you think that similar results would be obtained if the teachers were part of 'the largely European American teaching force', rather than Native American Indians?
- Can you think of rituals that bring together children, parents, teachers and the broader community in an early childhood education and care setting that you know?

Points to Discuss with another adult

- Do you think that early childhood staff would be more comfortable involving parents if they did not have to adhere to a 'fixed or static curriculum'?
- Do you think that the teachers in the article felt that their status as professionals was compromised by involving parents in their programme as closely as they did?

Research Snippet 2: Excluded parents: the deracialisation of parental involvement (Crozier, 2001)

Crozier (2001) undertook a detailed review of the place of 'race' in research on parent involvement in education in the UK. The excerpts below are from this research.

Some key findings

The blanket assumption that all parents are the same, with the same needs, and that their children can be treated in the same way is disturbing for all parents and particularly those who are already disadvantaged. With respect to ethnic minority parents, specifically, such an approach obfuscates the importance of tackling the nature and consequences of structural racism. At best, if racism is alluded to at all, it is merely reduced to an explanation of personal prejudice.   (Crozier, 2001: 330)

I do not want to set up misleading dichotomies or an essentialist argument ... (but) ... I do want to focus on ethnic minority parents here in order to attempt to critique the deracialisation of parent involvement policies ... It is my argument here that parental involvement policies are flawed in their failure to recognise the ethnic diversity amongst parents together with institutional racism within the education system.

(Crozier, 2001: 330)

Parental involvement in the normative sense is, in fact, underpinned by the specification of the "good" parent ... (and) ... where parents are not "good", then they need to be brought into line through, for example, parenting classes ... the "good" parent also remains unspecified (but) there is an implication that the "good" parent can be equated with being white and middle class ... (and) ... ethnic minority parents are generally not perceived as "good". Indeed, the research demonstrates a series of negative and stereotypical views of ethnic minority parents held by teachers.   (Crozier, 2001: 333)

Points to Ponder

- What do you think that Crozier means by 'institutional racism within the education system'? Have you seen any examples of it?
- What do you think is the difference between 'structural racism' and 'personal prejudice'? Why and to whom is the difference important?

Points to Discuss

- In your experience, do you think that 'the good parent' is generally white and middle class?
- In your experience, do teachers welcome any and all form of parent involvement in their child's education?

Fairness Alerts

The story and research we reviewed include examples of an unfair thinking habit called 'homogenizing'. Homogenizing assumes that all members of a particular group (e.g. a gender, a class, an ethnicity or a culture) are the same, thereby eradicating the perfectly normal and usual differences between people who are in the same group. In staff–parent relationships, each group can homogenize the other. In this chapter, we focus on how parents and staff can homogenize each other:

- Parents and staff can homogenize each other by thinking, 'They're all like that'.

Here is an example of homogenizing from the story:

Tanya: Well, I thought we might have a Chinese theme in the room for the first week or so. That might be a good way to show Min and her family that we respect their culture.

Trish: Yes, that would be fun. Maybe we could have some Chinese food so she has something that is familiar to her?

Jo: Do you know what her favourite foods are? I think her mother said she really likes pasta.

Trish: How funny, that's not really part of her culture is it? She's lucky to have a culture with such great food. I really like Chinese food.

Tanya: It will be good to do some cultural things with Min. We don't really do many cultural things. I might learn some Chinese songs and I think I saw a story about a Chinese girl with a duck or something – 'Ping' I think it was called – at the back of the cupboard.

Here is an example of homogenizing from the research around diverse cultural groups in early childhood education and care. It comes from a longitudinal action research study in the USA (Rothstein-Fisch et al., 2009) in which teachers working in primary schools 'used a cultural framework (individualism-collectivism) to understand differences between the culture of immigrant Latino families and the culture of US schools' (Rothstein-Fisch et al., 2009: 474). The aim of the project was to assess the value of the cultural framework of individualism and collectivism in the teachers' work. The following quote is the authors' explanation of the cultural framework given to the teachers.

Cultures that give priority to the needs of the individual – such as independence, freedom of choice, self-expression and private property – can be described as "individualistic". Those that give priority to the needs of the family or group, such as social relationships, group success, group consensus, respect and shared property can be described as "collectivistic". The dominant culture of the United States is highly individualistic. In contrast, many of the cultures of the most recent immigrants to the USA, as well as those of its indigenous peoples and many others, are highly collectivistic. This is true of Latin American cultures, Asian cultures and African cultures in general.   (Rothstein-Fisch et al., 2009: 475)

Why homogenizing is unfair

- People from any culture are complex individuals. Despite their shared cultural background, their experiences (e.g. of education) will not necessarily be the same.
- People within a particular culture (including you) will have had different experiences (e.g. of education).
- Researchers may find broad trends (e.g. attitudes to education) in a culture, but not every individual in that culture will conform to those broad trends.

How you can counter homogenizing

- Assume that people from different cultures may have had different experiences that may affect their attitudes to, for example, education.
- Be prepared to learn about the specific ways in which each family sees its children's education.
- Look for statements or actions that homogenize a group of people (e.g. a culture, a racial group) and challenge them.

Points to Ponder

- How would you distinguish between making broad, general statements about a group and homogenizing it?
- Can you explain in your own words why we think the conversation between Trish, Jo and Tanya (in the story) involved unfair thinking habits?
- In your experience of early childhood education and care, does it emphasize individualism or collectivism?

Points to Discuss

- Do you think that cultural difference is an issue in every early childhood education and care setting? How did you come to your conclusion?
- In your experience, are all people with Asian and African backgrounds 'collectivistic'?

Models of culture in staff–parent relationships

Culture is a complex concept with many different meanings. Many people define a culture in terms of what the people in that culture *do* – 'What do they eat?', 'What do they wear?', 'What sports do they play?' This reduces a culture's complexities to a tick-list – the sort of 'must see/do' list you would find in a tourist guide. It is not uncommon for well-intentioned early childhood staff to adopt such a 'tourism' attitude to ethnic or cultural difference in their centre. They acknowledge a culture other than their own by including some tokens of it in their programme, such as a special day, a special story or a special picture. This is a start, but it does not explore the different ways of seeing and ways of being that are associated with different cultures.

Exploring different models can help you to clarify what culture means to you and therefore how cultural respect can be practised in early childhood education and care settings. Our first model – culture as a way of seeing the world – is taken from the study by McCreery et al. (2007) of why Muslim parents in the UK want Muslim faith schools. In a wide-ranging analysis of their data, the researchers explore the implications of their findings for early childhood education and care preservice courses and for their views on diversity, parental rights and the role of education in society. The second model – culture is something to be absorbed – derives from a study by Mevorach (2008) of 18 Israeli preschool teachers who were from the mainstream cultural group teaching children from that group and from Ethiopian immigrant families. The focus of the study was the mental models that teachers had of children's learning. Mevorach argued that when teaching culturally diverse children, culture is an important dimension in teachers' models of children's learning.

The two models are followed by some 'Points to Ponder' and some 'Points to Discuss', which may help you decide what you think about how Trish, Jo and Tanya (in the story) saw culture – their own and Min's.

Model 1: Culture is a way of seeing the world

As educationists we are challenged by a different value system and a different way of being in the world. We can of course learn as much as we can about a different way of seeing the world, but ultimately we may not agree with it and we may not be comfortable with children being educated in such a way. . . . If we are to begin to understand the need for Muslim parents to provide their children with an education outside mainstream British schools, we must begin to confront these challenges and enter into dialogue so that we can understand our own perspective better and begin to understand what it is like to see the world from a Muslim point of view (Coles, 2004).   (McCreery et al., 2007: 217)

Model 2: Culture is something to be absorbed

We believe that culture is initially part of the external environment and becomes part of the child's inner world by means of cultural tools (Vygotsky, 1978). Therefore, we can assume that children from Ethiopian families approach mainstream preschool with a sense of bewilderment as regards proper cultural behavior and expectations. To compound this uncertainty, preschool teachers who are not aware of their children's cultural confusion misinterpret their behavior, thereby triggering the young child's low cognitive achievement from an early age. . . . Teachers' descriptions of how they teach children from cultural backgrounds that differ from the mainstream included an additional aspect that we defined as a metacategory called "culture". This category (sic) includes several special aspects (subcategories) such as cultural group, cultural style, relation to authority, level of learning, and everyday environment.   (Mevorach, 2008: 154)

Points to Ponder

- In each model, where is culture located?
- Is culture simply 'an additional aspect' of teachers' mental models of learning or something bigger?
- Can you see any links between these two models of culture and the models of culture that Jo, Trish or Tanya (in the story) expressed?

Points to Discuss

- Do you think that each culture should run its own, exclusive early childhood settings? How do you think that Jo (in the story) would answer that question? Why?
- If a culture is a way of seeing and being in the world, can we ever truly know a culture other than ours?

Further reading to deepen your understanding

Rothstein-Fisch, C., Trumbull, E. and Garcia, S.G. (2009) Making the implicit explicit: supporting teachers to bridge cultures. *Early Childhood Research Quarterly*, 24: 474–86.

Rothstein-Fisch et al. (2009) report on a research project in the USA, in which elementary teachers used an 'individualism–collectivism' dichotomy to explore differences between immigrant Latino students and the culture of their schools in the USA. At the start of the project, teachers were more likely to value individualism and by its end, they also valued collectivism; and they began to realize that a belief about education that is different to theirs is not necessarily wrong!

Koh, M.-S., Shin, S., Chung, I. and Reeves, K. (2009) Voices and culturally and linguistically diverse parents: a story of Korean parents of preschools. *Michigan Academician*, XXXIX: 11–29.

Koh et al. (2009) describe a study of how Korean immigrant parents in the USA with children in preschool maintain their children's cultural and linguistic heritage. It provides insights into how this group of immigrant parents see their own role and that of the preschool in preparing their children for their first formal year of schooling and the role of parents and preschools in maintaining Korean culture and heritage. It offers a useful point for reflection on the different ways in which parents see the role of preschools in maintaining their children's cultural traditions and language.

References

Crozier, G. (2001) Excluded parents: the deracialisation of parental involvement. *Race, Ethnicity and Education*, 4(4): 329–41.

Gilliard, J. and Moore, R. (2007) An investigation of how culture shapes curriculum in early care and education programs on a Native American Indian reservation. *Early Childhood Education Journal*, 34(4): 251–8.

Koh, M.-S., Shin, S., Chung, I. and Reeves, K. (2009) Voices and culturally and linguistically diverse parents: a story of Korean parents of preschools. *Michigan Academician*, XXXIX: 11–29.

McCreery, E., Jones, L. and Holmes, R. (2007) Why do Muslim parents want Muslim schools? *Early Years*, 27(3): 203–19.

Mevorach, M. (2008) Do preschool teachers perceive young children from immigrant families differently? *Journal of Early Childhood Teacher Education*, 29(2): 146–56.

Rothstein-Fisch, C., Trumbull, E. and Garcia, S. G. (2009) Making the implicit explicit: supporting teachers to bridge cultures. *Early Childhood Research Quarterly*, 24(4): 474–86.

7 Disclosing personal details – who needs to know?

To help you quickly grasp who's who, practitioners' names are shown in upright font and parents' names are shown in *italic* font.

Lena has reflected a lot on her work with parents and so Irena – the co-ordinator of her children's centre – has asked her to talk about her ideas at a weekly staff meeting. Lena has agreed, but has said to Irena, 'I'm not doing a speech or anything, right?' She need not have worried – as soon as she started talking, her ideas sparked lots of discussion!

> Irena: As you know, Lena is very interested in how we get along with the parents and has some ideas about this. I've asked her to share her thoughts with us today, because I know that our relationships with parents can sometimes be a bit stressful and we'd welcome any ideas about how to make things easier. So, over to you, Lena.
>
> Lena: Well, I guess the first thing I'd like to say is that we all expect parents to tell us about their children's family life, because we think that we can't really understand a child without it, don't we?
>
> Maria: I think this year . . . lots of parents are really open and willing to talk in detail, they're comfortable enough to come in and sit down and chat about the children, and I find that . . . it helps me and my job and, yeah, it makes life easier if I understand what's going on at home with the children and can help the children during their day with me.
>
> Lena: That's right. We say that parents should tell us about their families, but I think parents – well, some parents – think that sort of thing is personal and private, so they can find our expectations a bit hard.
>
> Zheng: I guess it's a bit of a trust thing too, where we're trusting them and they're trusting us, so part of the building up of a relationship

with us is that element of trust. The parents are writing very personal understandings and beliefs about who they are, as well, and so I think there is a respect element of, you know, privacy, too.

Irena: Of course, the accreditation schemes say that we should include parents in our decisions, but parents often think that we're 'the experts' and so they should leave those decisions to us.

Lena: Yes, and I don't like that. I don't see myself as the expert on other people's children.

Maria: Yeah, we're partners with parents. No-one knows everything, do they?

Lena: Hmmm. Well . . . I'm not sure about that. I'm not saying I'm the expert, but I don't think that I always include parents in my decisions. I don't always ask them what they think, or what they'd do in my place. And sometimes I just don't have time to listen to what a parent's saying, or I can't do anything about it just then. Time is always an issue. So, sometimes, I think, we say to parents, 'Please tell us what you think and what you want' and, 'Please tell us about your home and your family', but then when they do, we don't always listen to them.

Zheng: I don't know about that. I always try to listen to the parents . . .

Lena: Yes, we all do, but it just isn't possible to listen to every parent every time they want to talk. And this puts them off. So when we ask them about something, they don't always say what they think, because they think that if they criticise anything it'll make life harder for us.

Irena: Oh, I'm not sure about that, Lena.

Lena: Well, think about the *Parent Information* forms. When we give them out, we say that the information can help us to educate and care for their children. But some parents might not want to share that sort of personal stuff – I'm pretty sure I wouldn't!

Irena: I know what you mean. I was in a training session a while ago. There were twelve of us and when the facilitator asked us whether we tell parents about our families, five people said, 'Oh, we never disclose personal information to the parents – it's unprofessional.'

Lena: I used to think that when I gave one of our *Parent Information* forms to a parent I was saying, 'I value what you know about your child'. But actually I'm telling them what I think I need to know to make my job easier. And we don't really give them a choice, do we? It's, 'Oh, can you fill-in this form, please'.

Zheng: So do you think we shouldn't ask parents anything, Lena? I don't think that's right.

Maria: Yeah – how can we look after the children if we don't know anything about their backgrounds?

Lena: I'm not saying that we shouldn't ask them anything. I'm saying that we shouldn't ask questions about private things that make them feel uncomfortable. Why should we expect them to tell us personal stuff 'in the interests of the child'? Who really benefits when they do? I'm thinking that maybe we should ask them something like, 'What do you want to share with us?' or 'What do you think I should know about your child and do you mind telling me?' and we should make it clear that it's voluntary.

Zheng: Oh well, if you're going to do that, Lena, why not just give parents a blank piece of paper and ask them to write what they like!

Lena: I actually think that's a good idea! Let's try it and see what they say and see if we're any better or worse off.

Resources for thinking and talking about staff–parent relationships

Research Snippets

Here are two snippets from the research that concern how staff learn about 'personal stuff in the interests of the child' and what they do with such confidential information. Research Snippet 1 is taken from De Gioia (2009). The researcher did not study confidentiality issues directly, but found that parents often failed to disclose information about their child's home. Staff responses to parents' failure to disclose suggest that they had not asked parents the sort of open-ended questions that Lena advocated, such as 'What do you want to share with us?' or 'What do you think I should know about your child and do you mind telling me?'

Research Snippet 2 comes from a study by Clopton and East (2008) of children with a parent in prison. The topic may seem too specific to be helpful in **early childhood education and care settings**, but the article raises broad questions, similar to those raised by Maria, Lena, Zheng and Irena in the story: What right do early childhood education and care professionals have to inquire into a child's home? What does a teacher need to know about a child's life and background?

Following each Research Snippet are some 'Points to Ponder' and some 'Points to Discuss', which may help you decide if you agree with Lena (in the story) that Zheng's frustrated suggestion 'Why not just give parents a blank piece of paper and ask them to write what they like!' was, indeed, a good idea.

Research Snippet 1: Parent and staff expectations for continuity of home practices in the child care setting for families with diverse cultural backgrounds (De Gioia, 2009)

De Gioia (2009) used semi-structured interviews to explore whether staff working with children under three years of age in three **long day care** centres in Western Sydney (Australia) maintained the sleeping and eating habits that the children had developed at home; and how parents responded when staff introduced their children to sleeping and eating habits that differed from those at their home.

Some key findings

The staff

- All staff said that they tried to maintain continuity when parents gave them the information and that they try to negotiate any discontinuity. For example:

  . . . at home he gets Asian food every day and so I just tell his daddy maybe try to bring his own lunch (as the centre provides hot lunches daily for all children) and then we warm it up for him at lunch time. (Fran, untrained)   (De Gioia, 2009: 13)

- Seven staff had difficulty obtaining information from parents – beyond the enrolment form – about their child's sleeping and eating habits. For example:

  It has been really difficult to get our parents to tell us what they are doing at home. We did have a meeting a couple of weeks ago where we had eight parents come, but none of these parents put forward anything that they were doing at home that they wanted us to continue doing here at the centre, so we are really in a bind with that at the moment because if parents aren't willing to share, then it is hard for us to do it. (Lila, trained)   (De Gioia, 2009: 12–13)

- Some staff inquired about sleeping and eating habits at home and tried in various ways to replicate them, but eventually they adopted practices that they concealed from parents. They did so for two main reasons. First, some parents were reluctant to talk about their children's home. Five staff members were frustrated by that lack of information. For example:

They do not tend to tell us or give us any suggestions about how they do it at home, even if we do ask them. (Andrea, a Director).

(De Gioia, 2009: 14)

The second reason for concealing practices from parents was, simply, that the dominant culture triumphed. For example:

John used to be wrapped up and you know how big he is, like seven months, eight months, and she'd still want us to wrap him up and we said, "Oh look, we're not doing that because he's big enough and he can sleep fine without being wrapped up". (Margaret, trained)   (De Gioia, 2009: 14)

The parents

- Most parents said that staff–child ratios made it impossible for staff to follow the home practices of every child in their care.
- Some immigrant parents saw the centre as offering experiences and language that they could not offer at home.
- Four parents said that they thought it inappropriate for the centre to inquire about their child's home life.

Points to Ponder

- What did the research reveal about how staff and parents feel about sharing personal information?
- How could the staff have responded to the parents who were reluctant to talk about their family?

Points to Discuss

- In the light of Research Snippet 1, do you agree with Zheng (in the story), who believes that staff have a right to ask a family for personal information, because it can help them to work more effectively with their child?
- In the light of Research Snippet 1, do you think that staff can act in a child's best interests without knowing about their family? Would Maria (in the story) agree?

- In your experience, are some parents more likely than others to believe that staff can understand their child sufficiently without knowing about their family?

Research Snippet 2: 'Are there other kids like me?' Children with a parent in prison (Clopton and East, 2008)

Clopton and East (2008) reviewed the US research literature about children under five years old and in school settings who have a parent in prison.

Some key findings

- In 1999, an estimated one in fifty children in the USA had a parent in prison; and one in five of these children were under five years old.
- More recent statistics from elsewhere suggest that those figures will have increased. In 2006, 0.8 per cent of children under 18 years old in England and Wales had a parent in prison; and in 2003, around 38,500 children in Australia had a parent in prison (Rosenberg, 2009).
- Many educators may not be aware that a child has a parent in prison, as Clopton and East (2008: 197) explain:

Not all children and their caretakers are open about the incarceration of the parent (Davies et al. 2008; Nesmith and Ruhland, 2008). As a result educators may not be aware that a student has a parent in prison. In other cases an educator may be aware of the parent's incarceration, but the absence may not be discussed by the child or the caretaker. Educators need to be respectful of the caretaker's preferences regarding the issue; if the parent's incarceration becomes an issue at school, educators should communicate with the caretaker. The development of trust between the educator and the caretakers is important (Christian 2006). Moreover, some caretakers may welcome the support and opportunity to discuss the child's needs (Adalist-Estrin, n.d.).

(Clopton and East, 2008)

Points to Ponder

- Who should decide if early childhood staff need to know that a child has a parent in prison – the parent, the child, the early childhood staff, the justice system? Why do you think this? Would Maria and Zheng (in the story) agree with you?
- If you knew that a child in your care had a parent in prison, would it change your attitude and behaviour towards them?

Points to Discuss

- In the light of Research Snippet 2, do you believe staff in **early childhood services** have a *right* to know that a child in their care has a parent in prison? Why do you think this?
- Would it *help* staff in early childhood services if they knew that a child in their care has a parent in prison? Why do you think this?
- How would Lena (in the story) answer these questions?

 **Fairness Alert**

The story and the research literature we reviewed include some examples of an unfair thinking habit called 'privileging' – giving more weight to one set of views or experiences over any others. Here we explore how privileging ideas about what staff need to know about children can be an unfair thinking habit:

- Privileging staff views of what staff need to know about children over the views of their parents.
- Privileging the idea that staff have a right to know what children do at home over the idea that families have a right to privacy.

Here is an example of privileging from the story:

> Lena: Well, I guess the first thing I'd like to say is that we all expect parents to tell us about their children's family life, because we think that we can't really understand a child without it, don't we?

Lena: I used to think that when I gave one of our *Parent Information* forms to a parent I was saying, 'I value what you know about your child'. But actually I'm telling them what I think I need to know to make my job easier. And we don't really give them a choice, do we? It's, 'Oh, can you fill-in this form, please'.

Zheng: So do you think we shouldn't ask parents anything, Lena? I don't think that's right.

Maria: Yeah – how can we look after the children if we don't know anything about their backgrounds?

Here is an example of privileging from the research literature. It comes from an extremely powerful story of the efforts of an immigrant single-parent Latina mother living in California (Ramirez, 2005) to gain specialist language support for her daughter. The quote is taken from part of her story at the point at which a meeting she had struggled to get with the principal was postponed. To attend the meeting, she had taken a day off work that she could ill afford. Here is what happened to her:

The meeting with the principal and teacher did not go well. Although Esperanza showed up at the right time, the meeting was postponed due to a "clerical" error. Esperanza brought a note stating the date and time for the meeting, but the secretary had scheduled the meeting for another day. The school did not phone Esperanza about the mix-up, so she missed a day's wages and would miss another day's earning in order to come again, but was told by the school secretary regarding Esperanza's dilemma of missing another day of work, "Mrs. Marquez, you should be able to make a meeting that concerned your daughter . . . and as far as I could tell, your daughter needs a lot of help."

Esperanza felt as if someone had punched her in the stomach. She would have to miss another day of work, plus, the secretary seemed to indicate that she knew what the meeting was about. This breach of confidence and trust from the teacher and administrator made Esperanza even more frustrated. Esperanza shared with me that in her culture, matters concerning education and a student are kept confidential between the teacher and the parent. Personal histories or stories are never to be shared nor discussed with others, unless there has been permission to do so. Esperanza eventually did meet with the teacher and principal. During the meeting, the teacher and principal told Esperanza that her daughter was "not following directions," "turning in incomplete work," and "speaking to her friends in Spanish" after the teacher had told them not to speak in Spanish.   (Ramirez, 2005)

Why privileging is unfair

- It assumes that staff – because they are professionals – have a right to know personal information about the lives of children and their families.
- It implies that parents who do not disclose personal information do not know what is best for their child/ren and/or are 'bad' parents or unreasonable in seeking confidentiality.

How you can counter privileging

- Assume that parents and early childhood education and care staff have a right to privacy and a right to choose what to share.
- Do not assume that 'good' parents should disclose personal information to staff.
- Regard differences in opinions (e.g. about privacy and confidentiality) between staff and between staff and parents as normal and desirable.
- If you are a staff member, explain to parents why you are requesting family information and, if they are reluctant to give it, ask them to explain why. Actively encourage parents to tell you what they do and do not want to say about their family and show how such information can improve your care and education of their children.
- If you are a parent, ask staff why they want the information about your family that they are requesting and how it will improve the care and education of your children.
- If you are a student, look for and document examples of openness around requests for information and explanations.

Points to Ponder

- To which gender, class, ethnic or cultural groups do you belong? Have you (or someone you know) experienced 'privileging'?
- How might a family's circumstances influence their response to Lena's statement (in the story) that, 'we all expect parents to tell us about their children's family life'? For example, how might a family feel about their privacy if they are homeless, or poor, or experiencing violence or drug abuse? What did this expectation mean for Esperanza (in the research)?

Points to Discuss

- Have you seen/heard a particular type of knowledge being 'privileged' over others? How will you respond if you have a similar experience?
- Should parents and staff have the same rights to privacy? To what extent did the school secretary have a right to know about Esperanza's meeting (in the research) with the principal and why it was occurring? To what extent do you share Esperanza's approach to confidentiality?

Models of staff–parent relationships around privacy and confidentiality

There are several different ways to think about the place of privacy and confidentiality in staff-parent relationships. Lena, Maria and Zheng (in the story) each felt that knowing about a child's home life helped them do their job; but at the same time Lena and Irena were concerned how parents feel about disclosing such personal and private information.

Below are two contrasting models of families and privacy. Model 1 underpins an Australian research project (Imtoual et al., 2009) in which parents talked about their families in informal conversations. Model 2 appears in formal guidelines governing information about the families of children in services run by the Toronto Children's Services (TCS, n.d.). The models are followed by some 'Points to Ponder' and some 'Points to Discuss', which may help you decide what you think about the different attitudes to privacy expressed by the characters in the story.

Model 1: Families have a right to break the 'cycle of silence'

In our conversations it became apparent that the staff at the kindergarten value the practice of yarnin'. Yarnin' is an Aboriginal–English term that indicates informal but meaningful conversation. It is about sitting together and sharing stories, histories, advice, laughter and tears, and implies both active speaking and active listening. It is more than telling or retelling stories (personal stories, family stories, community stories); it is a transactional activity that involves negotiation and trust. It is democratic insofar as the stories are offered, but there is no compulsion to accept or act on what is spoken.

However, through yarnin', relationships, and indeed communities, are built and reinforced. Yarnin' is a space where thoughts and ideas can be shared and tested without shame. . . . At the **kindergarten** there is an explicit understanding that silence is linked to shame and a feeling of 'powerlessness' (Vallance and Tchacos, 2001). Yarnin' breaks the cycle of silence and shame through acknowledging that difficult issues need to be confronted and solutions worked out in supportive networks. (Imtoual et al., 2009: 27–8)

Model 2: Families have formal rights to silence

Parents/guardians should be aware that they have the authority to grant permission, or to refuse to grant permission, for the sharing of relevant information regarding their child. Clear procedures for ensuring confidentiality and the appropriate sharing of information in your policy statements or parent handbook will help establish trusting relationships. Procedures should be carefully explained and consistently followed, including a description of the measures that may be taken if there is a breach of confidentiality or inappropriate information sharing. (TCS, n.d.: 1)

Points to Ponder

- Which model is closer to your own view about parents' privacy?
- In the story, which staff member would feel most comfortable with the yarnin' model and which with the guidelines model?

Points to Discuss

- What model of parents' privacy do you have? How do your models resemble each other? How do they differ?
- How has your model of parents' privacy influenced your relationships in early childhood education and care settings?

Further reading to deepen your understanding

Swick, K. and Bailey, L. (2004) Communicating effectively with parents and families who are homeless. *Early Childhood Education Journal*, 32(4): 211–15.

Swick and Bailey (2004) propose an 'assets' approach to communication, in which parents tell early childhood staff about their strengths and then work with staff to organize resources and strategies that build on these strengths. An 'assets' approach emphasizes parents' right – irrespective of their circumstances – to shape their child's early education and life experiences. In contrast, a 'deficits' approach identifies what parents lack and tries to fill the gap. You could use this article to reflect on whether and how an 'assets' approach to communication between parents and staff in an early childhood education and care setting that you know could help Zheng (in the story) to build trusting relationships with parents.

Tomlin, A. and Hadadian, A. (2007) Early intervention providers and high-risk families. *Early Child Development and Care*, 177: 187–94.

Tomlin and Hadadian (2007) surveyed 146 early intervention staff (primarily white) in the USA who worked with 'high-risk' families that included, for example, a parent with a mental illness or disability, with substance addiction or other medical problem, or in which there were marital problems, a parent in prison, or involvement with child protection agencies. The researchers asked staff what type/s of training would support them in their work with these families, especially when parents disclosed personal information on intimate aspects of family life. You could use this article to reflect on whether and how staff can educate and care successfully for children from such families without knowing their family background; and to reflect on how such families might respond to Maria's question (in the story) – 'how can we look after the children if we don't know anything about their backgrounds?'

Ramirez, A. (2005) Esperanza's lessons: learning about education through the eyes of the innocent. (Reaching out to families: parental participation.) *Multicultural Education*, 13(2), Expanded Academic ASAP. Web. 1 July 2010. Available at www.eric.ed.gov/ERICWebPortal/recordDetail?accno=EJ75.

Ramirez (2005) is an extremely powerful and compelling article to read. It shares a story in detail of the struggles of a Latina single mother living in California to gain specific language support for her daughter in her early years of schooling. It highlights poignantly how confidentiality and the right to know is culturally constructed and laden with emotion. It offers an excellent opportunity to reflect deeply on the question of who has a right to know what about the work and personal lives of families. It raises the important point that assuming we all share the same views and values about confidentiality and the right to know is highly problematic, especially in contexts where different cultures intersect.

References

Clopton, K. and East, K. (2008) 'Are there other kids like me?' Children with a parent in prison. *Early Childhood Education Journal*, 36(2):195–8.

De Gioia, K. (2009) Parent and staff expectations for continuity of home practices in the child care setting for families with diverse cultural backgrounds. *Australian Journal of Early Childhood*, 34(3): 9–17.

Imtoual, A., Kameniar, B. and Bradley, D. (2009) Bottling the good stuff: stories of hospitality and yarnin' in a multi-racial kindergarten. *Australian Journal of Early Childhood*, 34(2): 24–30.

Ramirez, A. (2005) Esperanza's lessons: learning about education through the eyes of the innocent. (Reaching out to families: parental participation.) *Multicultural Education*, 13(2): 47–51. Available online at www.eric.ed.gov/ERICWebPortal/recordDetail?accno=EJ75 (accessed 1 July 2010).

Rosenberg, J. (2009) *Children Need Dads Too: Children with Fathers in Prison*. Geneva: Quaker United Nations Office.

Swick, K. and Bailey, L. (2004) Communicating effectively with parents and families who are homeless. *Early Childhood Education Journal*, 32(4): 211–15.

Tomlin, A. and Hadadian, A. (2007) Early intervention providers and high-risk families. *Early Child Development and Care*, 177(2): 187–94.

Toronto Children's Service (TCS) (n.d.) Confidentiality and Information Sharing Guidelines for Early Childhood Programs. Toronto: Toronto Children's Services.

8 Welcoming parents . . . but not really in this space

To help you quickly grasp who's who, practitioners' names are shown in upright font and parents' names are shown in *italic* font.

The Ferntree centre prides itself on welcoming parents and it has a long list of specific ways in which parents are welcomed. Irma, the Director, is having an informal conversation about Ferntree's approach with three parents – *Jane, Carla* and *Gayle.*

Jane: When I first came here, I was a little taken aback that we weren't allowed access to the centre, but that's changed a little since that's been spoken about. . . . I really have had difficulty with, I suppose, getting in the door because I didn't understand the routine at first and the door was locked. That was daunting . . . and I was on the committee! So I was put off by that. And when my four-year-old, Sam, was asked by his nanna what happens when his mum and/or dad come to the kindergarten, he said, 'Oh, the teachers lock dad up.' . . . (Much laughter and Irma says, 'Oh dear . . .')

Jane: . . . because he'd see his dad outside waiting for the door to be opened for him.

Irma: It's difficult, isn't it, because the centre is basically designed around children, not around their parents.

Carla: Well that's right. The foyer's a bit of a physical block to entry. Maybe the staff could stand out into the foyer a little bit more, to chat to the parents or bring them into the centre at the end of the session and then explain something. Because now, parents aren't sure why this is happening or why what's happening and so we all chat about it together in the foyer.

Gayle: And the car park's another place like that. If you want a chat with the other mothers about anything – you know, if it's about you or your children – then it generally happens in the car park, because there isn't a space in the centre for that. You're always sort of snatching a few minutes on the edge of the children's space, taking up the children's time with staff.

Irma: It would be better if you raised your concerns with us, rather than with each other, because we can sometimes do something about it. You don't want to rely on foyer gossip or on the car park mafia, as I sometimes call them. If it's something private, we can always talk in the office . . .

Gayle: Well yes, but that's generally only when there's a problem with your child, or if you want to ask about what's normal behaviour for a four-year-old, or something like that. There's nowhere that you can just have a private chat about your child, or problems at home or something like that.

Carla: Well that's right. If there's something that my child or any other child has done, I'd like the teacher in charge to talk to me about it in private . . . not sort of shout it out from ten feet away. I just think it's respectful. It's happened to me. In front of all the other parents and children it was like, 'Can you put him in underpants, because he shouldn't be in these . . .' and I was really taken aback, I felt ashamed and his little face dropped . . .

Irma: I'm so sorry about that, *Carla*, that really shouldn't have happened. But, you see, if a staff member moves away from their room to talk to you, then someone else has to do their work as well as their own; and also it might break our ratio of staff to children that's part of the rules around our registration. So the staff can't always talk to you as much as they'd like and as much as you'd like; and we don't like that any more than you do. That's why we try to use our communication books, our newsletters and our displays as much as possible.

Gayle: But it's not really the same, is it? I mean, some parents can get what they want from the books and newsletters, but for others, it's not necessarily going to be about the things they care about, is it?

Resources for thinking and talking about staff–parent relationships

Research Snippets

Here are two snippets from the research about the power relations between parents and staff in early education and care settings. Research Snippet 1 is from a study of how teachers in Israel saw parents' increasing empowerment in education (Addi-Raccah and Arviv-Elyashiv, 2008). Research Snippet 2 is from a research project in Ireland concerning the potential of a parents' space in early education and care settings (Martin, 2003).

Following each research snippet are some 'Points to Ponder' and some 'Points to Discuss', which may help you to decide what you think about the space issues that *Jane*, *Carla* and *Gayle* (in the story) raised with Irma.

> **Research Snippet 1: Parent empowerment and teacher professionalism: teacher perspectives (Addi-Raccah and Arviv-Elyashiv, 2008)**

Addi-Raccah and Arviv-Elyashiv (2008) used in-depth interviews and policy analysis to explore the reactions of five female teachers working in schools with parents of high socio-economic status in Israel to what they saw as parents' increasing empowerment in education.

Some key findings

- The teachers wanted parents to be involved in school but not to interfere in their professional domain. Like any other professionals, these teachers were concerned about being treated with respect and recognition, so they tried to protect their professional discretion from parental intrusion and interference (Lareau, 2000; Smrekar, 1996). (Addi-Raccah and Arviv-Elyashiv, 2008: 405)
- Teachers differed as to how comfortable they felt with parent empowerment at their school. For instance:

Sally also mentioned the importance of transparency: "Any parent who wants to come to school can do so. I don't hide anything. Usually the classroom door is open. Nothing secret is going on. I don't hide anything from parents. Many parents do come in, enter the classroom. It has also happened that they come especially to check on me. They see how the children are quiet and working. Then they say, 'It's very nice and quiet.'" An element of teachers' policy of transparency is to invite parents to watch class activities. They thereby create an opportunity to display their professional skills to the parents, as Shirley mentioned: "The door is always open, if parents let me know, they can come to watch my lessons. I always invite them." In another part of the interview she added, "It was suggested by the school coordinator that we invite parents to observe our lessons. We had no choice. It was decided. I enjoyed it very much, I don't care because I know how I teach and in my opinion the children benefit from it. The parents gave me positive feedback and they liked being able to come and see their kids." By displaying their mastery in teaching, teachers may persuade parents that they can be trusted to deliver appropriate educational services. However, for this to work, according to our interviewees, they apparently must indeed prove themselves "good" teachers. In this respect, our teachers claimed that those who have confidence in their professional ability have nothing to be concerned about. Shirley said, "I'm not worried about parents seeing how I teach, I'm not afraid at all, because I know I come prepared. I know that I'm a professional and I know what I teach."

(Addi-Raccah and Arviv-Elyashiv, 2008: 407)

Points to Ponder

- Do you think that a teacher's confidence in their abilities affects how they feel about parents being in their classroom?
- Do you think that a designated space in the Ferntree centre (in the story) for staff-parent conversations would improve communication between staff and parents there?

Points to Discuss

- When should and should not parents be allowed into an early childhood classroom? How do you think that Irma (in the story) might respond to this question?
- Who should decide when parents should and should not be allowed into an early childhood classroom – staff, parents, policy-makers or children?

Research Snippet 2: Parents as Partners in Early Childhood Services in Ireland: An Exploratory Study (Martin, 2003)

As part of her research study, Martin (2003) asked 79 parents and 56 staff from early childhood education and care settings in Ireland about the value of a dedicated parents' space.

Some key findings

- Parents' views: Five (6.3 per cent) of the parents used a service in which there was a parents' room and 4 made use of it; 74 (93.7 per cent) parents used a service that lacked a parents' room and 26 of these parents said that they would use such a room if available. (One parent considered such a room a waste of resources.)
- Staff views: Six (11 per cent) staff worked in a service in which there was a parents' room; 22 (39 per cent) staff said that they would like a parents' room in their service; 28 (50 per cent) staff said that they would not like a parents' room in their service.

Points to Ponder

- Why do you think that half the staff said that they would not like a parents' room in their service?
- Who is affected most when a service lacks a parents' room? How do you think that *Carla* (in the story) would answer this question?
- Which parents are the most likely to catch staff attention in public spaces such as the foyer or the car park? Which are the least likely?

Points to Discuss

- Do you know an early childhood education and care service that has a parents' room? If yes, how is it used? If no, would a parents' room be a good addition to the service and how do you think that the staff would respond to it?
- Have you ever had your professional practice challenged? If you have, how did you respond? If you have not, why do you think that is?

Fairness Alert

When inadequate or inappropriate space in an early childhood education and care setting affects different people differently, space becomes a political issue. The story and the research have shown that any particular space can allow some voices to be heard more than others and this is an example of an unfair thinking habit called 'silencing' – making it difficult for an individual or a group to be seen and/or heard. Specifically, in this case we examine how the organization of physical space can silence people:

* Silencing parents by having no space for them to talk.

Here is an example of silencing from the story:

> *Carla:* . . . . The foyer's a bit of a physical block to entry. Maybe the staff could stand out into the foyer a little bit more, to chat to the parents or bring them into the centre at the end of the session and then explain something. Because now, parents aren't sure why this is happening or why what's happening and so we all chat about it together in the foyer.

Here is an example of silencing from research literature. It is from a small-scale UK study in which the researcher asked parents about their relationships with their child's **nursery school** and then their primary school at the end of their child's first year at primary school (Shields, 2009: 244). We quote from a selection of the parents' responses:

> "I kind of feel shut off until I go back and collect her . . ."
> "I'm a bit unsure about that . . ."
> "Everything seems a bit confusing . . ."
> "Sometimes I wonder . . . if [my child] even feels a bit tense herself . . ."
> "It's a bit more of a mystery to me now, the inner workings of it."
> ". . . none of the parents know what's going on. So we're just milling about not knowing what to do . . ."

One parent in the study described how he was physically excluded from the school:

> I was sort of told the gate's open for your kids to come in at quarter to nine . . . The classroom was locked at the time, so we sort of hung around outside, milling about, and then the teachers would show up just before nine, and then they'd open the doors, but the

kids weren't allowed in . . . [Later] they tell me, yes, the gate's open at quarter to nine, so you can come in on the school grounds, but the classroom stays locked until nine, the kids are to queue up outside the classroom, nursery kids are allowed in, reception kids have to wait outside in a line. So I thought, OK, I did two open days, an induction night, and I had an information pack, and I didn't know any of that stuff! And I thought that's practical stuff I would have liked to have known.   (Shields, 2009: 244)

Why is silencing unfair?

- It assumes/implies that parents' views don't matter and, therefore, that there is no need to ensure that parents can express them.
- It denies parents' right to information about their children's lives at school and about how the school works, instead making them depend on staff for such information.

How you can counter silencing

- Assume that each individual or group has valuable ideas and views.
- Be alert to any silencing of an individual or group and actively seek their ideas and views. Do not assume that you have made them feel able to say what they think – always ask.
- Actively create space/s where parents feel comfortable expressing their ideas and where their ideas are treated with respect. Do not assume that you have succeeded in doing so – always ask.
- Periodically review any information for parents and visitors to your centre to ensure that it is still a useful guide to how things work.

Points to Ponder

- How can you tell when you are (or are not) welcome somewhere?
- How could the school in Shields (2009) reorganize itself in light of the parents' comments? Do you think that the reorganization that you propose would meet the concerns of *Jane*, *Carla* and *Gayle* (in the story)?

Points to Discuss

- Do you know an early childhood education and care space that actively welcomes parents? What makes it welcoming?
- Do you agree with Irma (in the story) that early childhood education and care settings are 'basically designed around children, not around their parents'? If you agree, why do you think that the designs have excluded parents? If you disagree, why do you think that parents (e.g. *Jane*, *Carla* and *Gayle* in the story; the parents in Shields, 2009) felt excluded?

Models of staff–parent relationships around the organization of space

As can be seen in the story and in the research, the organization of space is more than just a design issue! Below are two similar models of the significance of space (and design) in early childhood education and care settings. Model 1 underpins the design of a Centre of Excellence in Wisconsin, USA that aims to be not just pleasant and welcoming, but also inclusive. Model 2 emerges from a study in Australia that explicitly addressed the potential inequities associated with the organization of space.

The models are followed by some 'Points to Ponder' and some 'Points to Discuss', which may help you decide what you think about the ideas raised by *Jane*, *Carla* and *Gayle* (in the story) about relationships between space and equity.

Model 1: Space can be welcoming and inclusive

At the Encompass Centre (Green Bay), parents and children are arriving on a snowy January morning. Gloves and mittens are pulled off in order to receive a cup of hot chocolate and a warm whole wheat muffin in a lobby that looks like a living room, with sofas and soft colors to highlight the pictures on the wall created by children. With an equally warm smile, a local nutritionist greets each person and hands each parent a simple recipe card for making the muffins at home, including an explanation of why they are nutritious as well as tasty. Children electronically sign in by scanning their personal barcode cards through a small box attached to a computer in the lobby, and proceed to their class rooms with a feeling of welcome and anticipation of another day of exploration and learning in a positive and safe place in the care of their teachers. Parents pause for a few minutes to chat with their child's teacher before hurrying off to work. They clearly seem to feel "at home" and welcome in every corner of the center.

To encourage family participation, the staff of Encompass Child Care has discovered that they must first make parents feel welcome and respected. In the center lobby and in each classroom there are comfortable spaces set aside for parents and other family members, with an array of books, games, and other resources to encourage adults to meet informally. Children's artwork is displayed on walls and bulletin boards throughout the centre. Parents look for their own child's "masterpiece" and children are often seen proudly showing their parents where to look. Parents are welcome to spend time in the classroom, observing or helping their child settle into morning routines.   (Hamilton et al., 2003: 229)

Model 2: The effects of space can be inequitable

Space, like time, is a political issue when the effects of inappropriate space differentially affect specific groups of parents, To see these effects, staff, parents and policy makers need to reflect on how space, and its design, allows some voices to be heard more than others.
(MacNaughton, 2004: 5–6)

Points to Ponder

- How much of the feeling of welcome at the Encompass Child Care Centre is due to the organization of space there?
- Which individuals or groups are most likely to be (a) advantaged and (b) disadvantaged by the organization of space in early childhood education and care settings?

Points to Discuss

- Do you think that an early childhood education and care setting that you know organizes its space in a way that is equitable? How did you reach your conclusion?
- What single feature in an early childhood education and care setting that you know allows, 'some voices to be heard more than others' (MacNaughton, 2004: 6)?

> **Further reading to deepen your understanding**

Powers-Costello, E. and Swick, K. (2008) Exploring the dynamics of teacher perceptions of homeless children and families during the early years. *Early Childhood Education Journal*, 36: 241–5.

Powers-Costello and Swick (2008) explore the impact of homelessness on families' experiences of early childhood education and care services. The article can help early childhood education and care settings to organize space in ways that promote a social justice approach to homeless families.

Read, M. (2003) Use of color in child care environments: application of color for wayfinding and space definition in Alabama child care environments. *Early Childhood Education Journal*, 30 (4): 233–9

Read (2003) shows how to structure and define space in early childhood education and care settings simply by using colour, rather than more expensive structural changes.

References

Addi-Raccah, A. and Arviv-Elyashiv, R. (2008) Parent empowerment and teacher professionalism: teachers' perspective. *Urban Education*, 43(2): 394–416.

Hamilton, M., Roach, M. and Riley, D. (2003) Moving toward family-centered early care and education: the past, the present, and a glimpse of the future. *Early Childhood Education Journal*, 30(4): 225–32.

MacNaughton, G. (2004) Children, staff and parents: building respectful relationships in New Zealand and Australian early childhood contexts – the Australian context. *Australian Journal of Early Childhood*, 29(1): 1–7.

Martin, S. (2003) *Parents as Partners in Early Childhood Services in Ireland: An Exploratory Study*. Dublin: Dublin Institute of Technology.

Powers-Costello, E. and Swick, K. (2008) Exploring the dynamics of teacher perceptions of homeless children and families during the early years. *Early Childhood Education Journal*, 36(3): 241–5.

Read, M. (2003) Use of color in child care environments: application of color for wayfinding and space definition in Alabama child care environments. *Early Childhood Education Journal*, 30(4): 233–9.

Shields, P. (2009) 'School doesn't feel as much of a partnership': parents' perceptions of their children's transition from nursery school to reception class. *Early Years*, 29(3): 237–48.

9 Ways to communicate . . . but don't ruffle their feathers

The story

To help you quickly grasp who's who, practitioners' names are shown in upright font and parents' names are shown in *italic* font.

The Jimbaru centre is in an area with a high degree of social and cultural diversity. Consequently, the centre works hard to promote communication between staff and parents. It uses newsletters, suggestion boxes, parent meetings, questionnaires, notes and coffee mornings (most staff use a combination); and the centre director Janine ensures that staff are at the door before and after each session to meet and greet parents. We join a parents' coffee morning attended by Janine, her deputy, Fiona and four parents – *Louise, Ananya, Vicky* and *Sally*.

> Janine: I think it's really important we have open communication with parents and you know, don't you, that you can discuss any thing about your children with us, but I'm not sure that that always happens in the best way. All we can do is keep working on it.
>
> Fiona: It's a bit difficult, because there's so many different views and ideas about things. The staff have certain ideas and then the parents have loads of different ideas. So what do you do? . . . (Sighs) . . . It seems you've got thirty sets of different backgrounds and you are saying one thing but it's perceived in – yep – thirty different ways.
>
> Janine: Yes, different people can sometimes have different interests at stake and in this centre we're dealing with people from all sorts of different cultural backgrounds and their different ideas and views. And when there is a dilemma about what different people want, there's no-one, really, to turn to.

Louise: Communication is encouraged, yes. There's the suggestion box and the meetings . . . but a lot of people wouldn't take it up. If I need to say something, I'll try to do it on the way out or on the way in – probably *not* on the way in. (Laughter)

Ananya: I think if you do want to say anything, you've really got to ring and deal with things afterwards, without sort of ruffling any feathers. That probably sounds really negative and I don't mean it like that . . .

Janine: Sorry, *Ananya*, but what do you mean – 'ruffling any feathers'?

Vicky: Well I can give you an example of that. Last year, you gave us a questionnaire to fill out about the centre. As far as I knew, it was anonymous and I filled it out. One question was something like, 'Do you know that you can see a progress report on your child at any time?' and I just circled 'No', because I didn't know that. Now, I don't know if it was marked so that you knew who answered, but fifteen minutes after I returned the questionnaire, I had a phone call telling me that I'm wrong – there *is* a progress report of my child and I *can* see it when I want to. So I'd clearly said the wrong thing there!

Sally: I think you've really got your hands full here and you've got to juggle lots of things, but some things aren't right for everyone but it's really hard to say anything. And the newsletters, the noticeboards and that are really good, but they're not . . . Look, there's just me and Ben, as you know, and on Fathers Day, everyone made cards, but Ben hasn't got a dad, so what's he going to do? I made a point of saying to him. 'You can make a card for Poppy – a Poppy's Day card.' I've had to force myself with things like that to protect him. . . . I know you do what you can, but there's some times like Fathers Day where perhaps you don't take that into account.

Louise: Come on, *Sal*, it's not that big a deal. If you hadn't said something, Ben probably wouldn't have noticed and just joined in. It doesn't *mean* anything.

Fiona: You'd find Fathers Day cards in any Australian children's centre or kindergarten. It's just part of Aussie culture, isn't it?

Janine: We probably could have handled that differently, *Sally*, but it is traditional to make cards on Fathers Day.

Ananya: Well, I know that it's part of being in Australia, but, um, I think it would be good if other cultures and traditions . . . but, you see, I might ruffle some more feathers now . . .

Janine: No, go on, *Ananya* – we'll keep our feathers on! (Laughter)

Ananya: (Silent)

Sally: I think I know where *Ananya's* coming from. If you're, like, part of the mainstream, then everything's fine, isn't it? There's no problem *because* you're in the mainstream. So if Fathers Day is just a normal part of being a typical Aussie and you're a typical Aussie, there's no need to ruffle any feathers about it, is there? But if it isn't part of your life, then either you just keep your head down or you get a reputation as 'one of *those* parents' – you're 'demanding' and . . .

Ananya: . . . and it's hard to speak up if your language isn't English, or if you're outside the main culture . . .

Sally: . . . or just if you're shy. Who gets heard when you have to be careful what you say? You're safe as long as you stay within the norm, but if you're outside . . .

Resources for thinking and talking about staff–parent relationships

Research Snippets

Here are two snippets from the research about tensions surrounding parents' involvement in their children's education. Research Snippet 1 is from a secondary school study in the USA (Vincent and Martin, 2002), but its findings are relevant to staff–parent relationships across educational settings, including early childhood education and care. Research Snippet 2 is from a small study of how **elementary school** students' parents – especially working class mothers – react to expectations that they should be 'involved' in their children's education (Freeman, 2009).

Following each Research Snippet are some 'Points to Ponder' and some 'Points to Discuss', which may help you decide what you think about the risks in the story of 'ruffling feathers' by challenging the consensus.

Research Snippet 1: Class, culture and agency: researching parental voice (Vincent and Martin, 2002)

Vincent and Martin (2002) explored the individual, institutional, material, social and cultural factors that influence how parents form and express their views in schools. The researchers conducted surveys and interviews among 20 teachers, 11 school governors and 61 families from diverse socio-economic backgrounds in two secondary schools.

Some key findings

In the main, 'high' parents asserted their own knowledge over professionals' only when severe welfare issues concerning their child arose (e.g. bullying, special needs; see Vincent and Martin, 2000). One mother whose child has Asperger's syndrome struggled to get the school to recognize and appreciate her son's difference:

> "I can understand why parents get that angry. Because I couldn't get them to see my point of view. . . . I said, 'You are not listening to what I am saying. This is a problem, it's not going to go away.' . . . I didn't feel like I was getting any help. It was like me and him against the world."
>
> (White mother, works in supermarket; the father clerk of works at council, Carson [school].)

Her words were echoed by two parents at Willow (school). Their daughter, who has dyspraxia, was being bullied at school:

> Mother: "You get this very defensive reaction. They don't like, it's almost saying 'We don't like you being this articulate and having the knowledge' because they don't have the upper hand."
>
> Father: "Teachers by their nature are a bit kind of authoritarian, because they're in a class getting 30 people to do what they want, and if parents don't do what they want, then they get a bit naffed off by that, you know, and I think they don't like people who actually say 'It's not quite like that, it's like this', you know."
>
> Mother: "I've absolutely no idea what I could do to change my approach and reaction, I don't know, I've got no ideas left. What can I do? I don't know." (White parents, mother TV producer, father surveyor, Willow.)   (Vincent and Martin, 2002: 118)

We uncovered considerable cynicism, especially from 'intermediate' and 'low' parents about the activities of the parents' forums, a feeling that such groups could engineer little change, and that, therefore, attending meetings was not a rational investment of time and effort.   (Vincent and Martin, 2002: 124)

. . . we conclude that parental voice in the schools we studied was most often individual, cautious and insecure, evidently lacking in a sense of entitlement to speak in the public arena of the school.

(Vincent and Martin, 2002: 125)

Points to Ponder

- To what extent would the researchers' findings be echoed in an early childhood education and care setting that you know? How did you reach your conclusion?
- In the story, which parents did and did not have 'a sense of entitlement to speak' (Vincent and Martin, 2002: 125)? What happened when *Sally* (in the story) spoke up about Fathers Day?

Points to Discuss

- Do you think that some people 'ruffle *your* feathers' (be honest!)? Why do you think this happens? Are you happy for it to continue to happen?
- Do you know of any parents who feel 'cautious and insecure' (Vincent and Martin, 2002: 125) about speaking out in their children's early childhood education and care setting? Why do you think this happens?

Research Snippet 2: 'Knowledge is acting': working-class parents' intentional acts of positioning within the discursive practice of involvement (Freeman, 2009)

Freeman (2009) conducted in-depth interviews with 11 parents from working- and middle-class backgrounds who had children at an elementary school in Georgia, USA. The topic was their experiences of parent involvement.

Some key findings

- The working-class parents in this study were very clear that parent involvement in their child's schooling was expected of them. However, to involve themselves in their children's school was not easy or straightforward. They had to challenge stereotypes that teachers held about their working-class background; work hard not to feel inferior to the teachers; and make a considerable effort to talk with the teachers and share their ideas, so that teachers could see that they held valid and valuable points of view. Teachers did not often respond positively or well to these conversations.

- Freeman concluded that critical conversations between teachers and working-class parents were essential to building positive and equitable relationships between them:

> . . . involving parents in critical conversations, whether during parent–teacher conferences or in open forums, does not thwart the need to continuously monitor how such conversations, or any form of involvement, function to oppress parents or create new forms of inequalities, especially since involvement already privileges those with power (Borg and Mayo 2001; Brain and Reid 2003; Vincent and Martin 2002). . . . (and) . . . assuming that creating the conditions for dialog is sufficient for dialog to occur undermines the way culture and positioning will not only affect the way parents participate but whether they will participate. It is important therefore to realize that enabling critical conversations between teachers and parents may be difficult to put into place, not only because of the resistance that may be exhibited by teachers, but also because some parents; for example, some Latinos or lower-class parents, may not be in the habit of questioning the authority of the teachers or may feel they have little to offer educationally. (Lareau and Shumar 1996; Marschall 2006).
>
> (Freeman, 2009: 195–6)

Points to Ponder

- Can you list some stereotypes about working-class parents that you might find in an early childhood education and care setting? Does any of them resonate with *Sally*'s statement (in the story) that, 'You're safe as long as you stay within the norm, but if you're outside . . .'?
- What do you think Freeman (2009) meant by 'critical conversations'? How could you use such conversations to challenge stereotypes about working-class parents?

Points to Discuss

- In your experience, do working-class parents feel inferior/subordinate to early childhood education and care staff sometimes? How might this influence how working-class parents react to expectations that they should be 'involved'?
- In your experience, what sorts of parent get involved in their children's education and which ones do not? Remember *Ananya*'s comment (in the story): '. . . and it's hard to speak up if your language isn't English, or if you're outside the main culture.'

Fairness Alert

In the story, everyone wanted good communication, but when *Sally* and *Ananya* raised their separate concerns about Fathers Day, they did not get very far. Instead, *Sally* and *Ananya* were victims of an unfair thinking habit called 'silencing' – making it difficult for an individual or a group to be seen and/or heard. We draw on that example to focus on how consensus can silence:

- Silencing parents by allowing no views outside the assumed consensus.

Here is an example of silencing from the story:

Sally: I think I know where *Ananya*'s coming from. If you're, like, part of the mainstream, then everything's fine, isn't it? There's no problem *because* you're in the mainstream. So if Fathers Day is just a normal part of being a typical Aussie and you're a typical Aussie, there's no need to ruffle any feathers about it, is there? But if it isn't part of your life, then either you just keep your head down or you get a reputation as 'one of *those* parents' – you're 'demanding' and. . . .

Ananya: . . . and it's hard to speak up if your language isn't English, or if you're outside the main culture. . . .

Sally: . . . or just if you're shy. Who gets heard when you have to be careful what you say?

Here is an example of silencing from the research about staff-parent communication. It is from an Australian study in which the researcher used focus groups to examined the extent to which parents believed that they had a partnership with early childhood staff in caring for their child (Elliott, 2003). The quote is from one of the parents who participated in that study:

> I don't feel that staff really listen to or answer your questions. I saw a computer timetable posted on the window showing when each child was to have time in the computer centre, my child's name was on the list for that day so I asked her if she had been playing on the computer. She said 'no'. So I asked the staff member how the roster worked and what were the children working on when having computer time, because I wanted to understand what they were teaching and the children were learning. The staff member talked but didn't actually answer the question. I gave up and the next day the roster was not on the wall. It had been taken down.   (Elliott, 2003: 19)

Why silencing is unfair

- It assumes/implies that one particular way to see things or do things is right – or at least is so dominant that it need not be questioned.
- It assumes that 'we're all the same' and 'we're all in this together' and that anyone who has a different perspective is a bit odd.
- It pretends that society is homogeneous, yet privileges mainstream views over other competing views.

How you can counter silencing

- Actively seek ideas and views about young children's education and care that are outside the mainstream.
- Actively create circumstances where holders of 'non-mainstream' views about young children feel comfortable expressing them and where their ideas are treated with respect. Do not assume that you have succeeded in doing so – always ask.
- Be prepared to rethink your ideas about young children's education and care if they fail to reflect the experiences of families with whom you work.
- If you encounter ideas and practices that you find unacceptable, explain your position, rather than just pretend that it isn't an issue . . . and be prepared to rethink your position if circumstances change.

Points to Ponder

- When *Sally* (in the story) heard that Fathers Day is 'just part of Aussie culture', do you think that this calmed her concerns about Ben's feelings?
- Is 'a typical Aussie' a valid description of real people or is it a stereotype that really fits no one?

Points to Discuss

- Do you think that all views about how to educate and care for young children are equally valid? If not, how do you decide which ones to ignore?
- In your experience, do people who hold mainstream views about how to educate and care for young children silence people who disagree with them?

Models of staff–parent relationships around consensus

The story and the research show that parents and staff can get on well if they stay within mainstream views of early childhood education and care and/or within the local consensus about how best to educate and care for young children. Below are two models of staff–parent relationships that differ markedly in their view of consensus. Model 1 emerged from a research study about teacher professionalism in urban primary schools in Israel (Addi-Raccah and Arviv-Elyashiv, 2008); Model 2 emerged from a US study of conflict in parent involvement (Freeman, 2009).

The models are followed by some 'Points to Ponder' and some 'Points to Discuss', which may help you decide what you think about the risks in the story of 'ruffling their feathers' by challenging the consensus.

Model 1: Good staff–parent relationships avoid conflict

Beth remarked, "I have a very clear strategy. I'm extremely connected to the children. . . . To avoid conflict with parents, I try to agree with them. . . . I try to have a friendly relationship with them, otherwise teaching is impossible. . . . I tend to please parents. I don't insist on everything. I'm friendly with them."

(T)eachers play the game; they fulfill parents' expectations to be caring, warm, and empathic to their children. The teachers also reported that they could single out parents who were most likely to make "trouble" and they tried to preempt this by treating their children more kindly and as favorites, for example, by altering grades or being friendlier with them. These hidden strategies mainly focused on particular children. In fact, it was clear that in handling a student, teachers also take her or his parents into account. Liz believed that "parents have an impact. . . . It's awful, but there are children who I assess more casually and others to whom I devote more thought about their grades because I know that the parent will be more attentive." Sally was quite clear about this too: "When I think about the kid I'm really thinking about his or her parents. . . . I'm very cautious. I think twice about what I do. . . . There's no doubt that the parents are very 'problematic'. You think twice about what you do."

Presumably, then, at the individual level teachers apply favoritism to avoid criticism and to mobilize parental approval and recognition, as suggested by Blasé (1988).

(Addi-Raccah and Arviv-Elyashiv, 2008: 409)

Model 2: Good staff–parent relationships invite difference

A dialogical view of parent–teacher communication offers a different conception of involvement, one that resists transmission. Although the working-class parents joked about being "demanding", they are not the kind of parents Casanova (1996) talks about who seek to control the curriculum for their children. Quite the contrary, the working-class parents' accounts suggest a very different conception of involvement, one that more closely fits Freire's (1970/1996) notion of collaborative problem-posing where people, in this case teachers and parents, come together as learners. Implementation of real conversations around concrete situations has the potential to encourage a co-constructed involvement that would be more inclusive of all parents. To be sure, different people may have different interests and bring different concerns and expertise to the table, differences of opinion and point of view will need to be facilitated and mediated, but as the working-class parents' accounts suggest, difficult conversations are not necessarily to be avoided.

(Freeman, 2009: 195)

Points to Ponder

- Do you agree with Beth (Model 1) that teaching is impossible without a friendly relationship with parents? How have you reached your conclusion?
- Do you agree with Freeman (2009) that, 'difficult conversations are not necessarily to be avoided'? Do you think that *Ananya* (in the story) would agree?

Points to Discuss

- In your experience, is avoiding conflict and tension in relationships a successful strategy? Do you think that it worked for Fiona (in the story)?
- In your experience, do individual teachers 'apply favoritism to avoid criticism and to mobilize parental approval and recognition'?

Further reading to deepen your understanding

Freeman, M. (2009) 'Knowledge is acting': working-class parents' intentional acts of positioning within the discursive practice of involvement. *International Journal of Qualitative Studies in Education*, 23(2): 181–8.

Freeman (2009) used extensive quotes to show how working-class mothers in the USA explain themselves and their actions within the particular discourse of parent involvement at their children's school. This is a school-based study, but it examines parents' experiences of being involved in their children's early years of schooling. This, plus its use of theoretical ideas about how parents react to expectations that they should be involved in their child's education, may deepen your understanding of parent involvement programmes – especially those in socio-economically diverse communities.

Freeman, N. and Swick, K. (2007) The ethical dimensions of working with parents: using the code of ethics when faced with a difficult decision. *Childhood Education*, 83(3): 163–9.

Freeman and Swick (2007) provide a series of ethical dilemmas that early childhood education and care staff may face in working with parents; and they explore how to use the National Association for the Education of Young Children (NAEYC) Code of Ethics to resolve those dilemmas ethically. The article offers helpful suggestions about responding in ethical ways to tensions and disagreements in staff-parent relationships.

References

Addi-Raccah, A. and Arviv-Elyashiv, R. (2008) Parent empowerment and teacher professionalism: teachers' perspective. *Urban Education*, 43(2): 394–16.

Elliott, R. (2003) Sharing care and education: parents' perspectives. *Australian Journal of Early Childhood*, 28(4): 14–21.

Freeman, M. (2009) 'Knowledge is acting': working-class parents' intentional acts of positioning within the discursive practice of involvement. *International Journal of Qualitative Studies in Education*, 23(2): 181–98.

Freeman, N. and Swick, K. (2007) The ethical dimensions of working with parents: using the code of ethics when faced with a difficult decision. *Childhood Education*, 83(3): 163–9.

Vincent, C. and Martin, J. (2002) Class, culture and agency: researching parental voice. *Discourse: Studies in the Cultural Politics of Education*, 23(1): 110–28.

10 I just want some feedback!

The story

To help you quickly grasp who's who, practitioners' names are shown in upright font and parents' names are shown in *italic* font.

For many early childhood staff, involving parents in their programme can be a major source of job satisfaction . . . or job frustration! Beverley is a researcher examining job satisfaction in early childhood services. Today she is visiting the Lonsdale centre and talking to centre director Ingrid and her deputy Sally.

Beverley: Do you believe that parents can affect your sense of job satisfaction?

Sally: Oh certainly. If feedback from parents, or lack of feedback (it's usually lack of feedback) – if you're not getting any pats on the back from parents, you can wonder what you are doing it for. But some parents *are* appreciative – they *do* make the effort to thank you for things and they *do* acknowledge the role you are playing in their lives and in their children's lives. They make the job much more satisfying.

Ingrid: I know that our parents – some of them – often think that they're asking too much, or that they're giving us a hard time when they need to re-arrange **occasional care** or change their hours. But in actual fact, that's not what's difficult with parents. It's the parents who really don't want to return any of the stuff that we give to them or to their children in the course of the day. The parents who don't share information can be difficult. And parents who are consistently late.

Sally: And it's the parents who just come in and dump their children and go and they treat you as a sort of babysitting service. And you start to think, well, 'What am I here for? Just what *is* my role here?' You get told one thing at college, but it's something else when you get here.

Ingrid: But you get some parents who come in and spend a little bit of time at the centre, which a lot of ours do, and interact with the girls and ask what they are doing and why, which I think is really important. The girls can go into the developmental reasons why they're doing this activity and not something else, so a lot of it is educating the parents, I think. We have talks about what the girls have been doing in their rooms, and why; and we have lots of posters up saying why we offer, like, sandplay – not just because it feels good, but there are other reasons.

Sally: Yes, a lot of the parents from this area came into childcare at the start of last year, but didn't really know what childcare was. They didn't know what to expect from it, they didn't know how they could be involved, so that was why we had a lot of social nights to get the parents in. That's been . . . they're getting more out of it themselves, and also it's a support link for them when they can come and talk to the staff and say, 'This happened last night . . . what do you think about it?' And there is a lot of feedback between each other, which has been very helpful to both parents and staff, I think.

Ingrid: So parent involvement is a big thing for us, but despite that, we have very modest expectations – we just want to tell parents about their child's day and to hear parents' concerns about their children.

Resources for thinking and talking about staff–parent relationships

Research Snippets

Here are two snippets from the research about parents' involvement in early childhood education and care programmes. Research Snippet 1 comes from a study of the barriers to parent involvement in Head Start programmes in the USA and shows that parents may have to balance involvement in their child's education and care programme with other demands on their time (Lamb-Parker et al., 2001). Research Snippet 2 is from a study in the USA that asked what influenced the quality of communication between parents, kindergarten teachers, preschool teachers and family workers (Rimm-Kaufman and Pianta, 2005).

Following each Research Snippet are some 'Points to Ponder' and some 'Points to Discuss', which may help you decide what you think about Ingrid's and Sally's expectations (in the story) of parents' involvement.

> **Research Snippet 1: Understanding barriers to parent involvement in Head Start: a research-community partnership (Lamb-Parker et al., 2001)**

Lamb-Parker et al. (2001) used a 'Barriers to Parent Involvement Survey' to interview 68 mothers in New York about factors that prevented them from getting involved in their children's education. Their children had attended one of two Head Start programmes for a year. One programme served primarily low-income Latino parents. The second programme was in a middle-income area and children from low-income African-American families came there by bus.

Some key findings

- The mothers faced many difficulties. For example, one-third of them said that they had no heat, hot water, or electricity during part of the Head Start year; and almost half-reported, 'often feeling sad, down, depressed'. Nevertheless, few mothers said that their circumstances were barriers to their involvement (Lamb-Parker et al., 2001: 45).
- . . . the major impediments to greater involvement involved prior commitments and scheduling conflicts. The results point to the need for Head Start programmes to modify some of their traditional parent involvement activities, such as volunteering in the classroom, to accommodate the mother's employment-related responsibilities (Lamb-Parker et al., 2001: 46).
- The survey results confirmed what Head Start agencies knew – that young mothers' time to participate in traditional parent involvement activities was limited because they had to enter job training or employment to meet 'welfare-to-work' requirements. One Head Start agency used the survey results to agree with local welfare-to-work programmes that the agency could be regarded as a work site, enabling mothers to meet their welfare-to-work requirements while they participated in Head Start activities (for example, classes in English as a Second Language, classes related to job interviews and resumes) (Lamb-Parker et al., 2001: 46).
- Several mothers said that language is a barrier to parent involvement. The staff at one Head Start agency helped one mother to

communicate more effectively, feel less isolated and increase her involvement in the Head Start programme by introducing her to a 'mentor parent' who spoke her dialect, but had not found that language impeded her involvement in the Head Start programme.

(Lamb-Parker et al., 2001: 47).

Points to Ponder

- Do you think that parents' domestic circumstances often affect their level of involvement with their children's education and care? Are all parents affected equally?
- If Ingrid and Sally (in the story) asked 'uninvolved' parents about their domestic circumstances, would this explain the variability in parent involvement? Do they have a right to ask such questions?

Points to Discuss

- In your experience, are 'prior commitments and scheduling conflicts' widespread and major barriers to greater parent involvement? Do you think that Ingrid and Sally (in the story) are aware of this possibility?
- Can you generate any creative solutions (equivalent to the 'mentor parents' in the study) to those barriers?

Research Snippet 2: Family-school communication in preschool and kindergarten in the context of a relationship-enhancing intervention (Rimm-Kaufman and Pianta, 2005)

In this longitudinal study in the USA, Rimm-Kaufman and Pianta (2005) used participant communication logs to capture 22,000 contacts between preschool and kindergarten teachers and family workers of 75 children from families with low socio-economic status.

Some key findings

- Communication between preschool staff and parents was greater than that between kindergarten teachers and parents:

  > Findings showed a decrease in family–school communication between preschool and kindergarten. Families of preschool children become accustomed to receiving information from their child's school as frequently as seven times per month, and this drops to 1.5 contacts per month upon the entrance into kindergarten.
  >
  > (Rimm-Kaufman and Pianta, 2005: 309)

- Family factors did not influence the nature of staff–parent communication significantly.
- Overall, in both settings (preschools and kindergartens) staff initiated contact more frequently than did the parents:

  > The majority of family–school contacts involved the child's mother and approximately two-thirds of the contacts were school-initiated, not home-initiated. Teachers reported having positive impressions of most of the communication with families in preschool and kindergarten. Between 25% and 55% of contacts were letters sent home to parents, and approximately the same percent of contacts were school visits. These findings showed few differences between contact in preschool and in kindergarten, a finding that contrasts with research showing that between preschool and kindergarten, families experience a decrease in home-initiated contacts, an increase in notes exchanged, and an increase in information exchanged about behavior and academic problems.
  >
  > (Rimm-Kaufman and Pianta, 1999, cited in Rimm-Kaufman and Pianta, 2005: 310)

Points to Ponder

- Why do you think that the staff in this research initiated communication with parents more often that parents did?
- Do you think that it matters who initiates staff–parent communication? How do you think that Ingrid and Sally (in the story) would each answer this question?

Points to Discuss

- In your experience, is information exchange between parents and staff different in different forms of education and care provision? Why do you think this is?
- In your experience, who generally initiates information exchange between staff and parents? Why do you think this is?

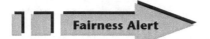 **Fairness Alert**

Research in the area of parent involvement can sometimes – and implicitly – be judgemental about parents who do not get involved in their children's education and care; and Ingrid and Sally (in the story) were certainly clear that some parents just did not meet their expectations of 'good' parents. These are all instances of an unfair thinking habit called 'othering' – seeing yourself and/or your group as the norm, from which everyone else deviates. Specifically, in this instance we have pointed to othering parents who do not participate.

Here is an example of othering from the story:

Ingrid: The parents who don't share information can be difficult. And parents who are consistently late.
Sally: And it's those parents who just come in and dump their children and go and they treat you as a babysitting service.

Our chosen example of othering from the research literature is from a review of research literature used at several points in this chapter about parents' attitudes to their children's teachers and schools (Knopf and Swick, 2006). The quote we use is not the authors' opinion but summarizes what other researchers have found.

Parents do not care. This stereotype is rooted in teachers' perceptions of what "caring" parents do to support their child's education and classroom functioning. . . . Teachers often perceive the failure of families to participate in parent/family involvement programs or in other school functions as supporting the idea that parents don't care. (Lawrence-Lightfoot, 2003, cited in Knopf and Swick, 2006: 293)

Why othering is unfair

- Assuming that parents *should* be involved means that any parent who cannot be involved or who believes that their involvement is unnecessary appears to be 'a bad parent'.
- A parent's lack of involvement can be a matter of their culture or ethnicity, not their conscientiousness. Cultures can differ in their view of parents' role in early childhood and care settings.
- Differences are just/only that – differences.

How you can counter othering

- List all the reasons (include positive ones) you can think of why a parent may not be involved in their child's programme.
- Use your list to spark discussions (with colleagues and parents) about parent involvement in your programme.
- Seek creative solutions to some of the barriers to involvement but remember – some parents (for whatever reason) do not want to be involved.

Points to Ponder

- Do you think that parents who do not initiate communication with early childhood education and care staff do not care about their child's education and care? How do you think that Ingrid and Sally (in the story) would each answer this question?
- Do you think that staff should initiate communication with parents who seem reluctant to comment about their child's education and care? Would the parents see this as intrusive?

Points to Discuss

- Do you believe that early childhood education and care staff have a responsibility to ensure good communication between staff and parents – including initiating it, if necessary?
- Is communicating fully with staff a mark of a good parent?

Models of staff–parent relationships around parents' lack of involvement

It is clear from the story and the research that there are widely differing views of parents' reasons for staying out of their children's education and care settings. Here are two models of parents' lack of involvement. Both start from the same point – some parents are uninvolved – but each model explains that lack of involvement differently and poses quite a different response to it. Model 1 emerged from a review of research in the USA into parents' attitudes to their children's teachers and schools (Knopf and Swick, 2006); Model 2 was developed from a review of parent–teacher relationships in the USA (Keyes, 2000).

The models are followed by some 'Points to Ponder' and some 'Points to Discuss', which may help you decide what you think about Ingrid's and Sally's expectations (in the story) of parent involvement.

Model 1 Staff can motivate parents to get involved in their programme

Parents do not have the time or motivation to be involved (Epstein, 1995). This stereotype, on the surface, seems to appreciate the busy and demanding responsibilities that parents face, while at the same time discounting the importance that the development of meaningful relationships may have in providing motivation and helping parents "find time" to get involved . . . Epstein (1995) also notes that when parents and families feel connected to the school they take the time to be involved. Caring behaviors of teachers can make a difference when, for example, teachers involve parents in the planning of activities and events, or use parent leadership as an educational tool to motivate and educate. Rich (1992) also found that when parents were asked to give input on ways they could be involved, their participation increased.   (Knopf and Swick, 2006: 294)

Model 2 Staff cannot motivate parents to get involved in their programme

From the teachers' perspectives, some feel unappreciated by parents. They say that parents don't come to conferences or meetings, don't read the material they send home, and won't volunteer for school activities. Some teachers feel that parents seem to lack interest in what's going on with their children. Others describe parents as adversarial or apathetic, always a challenge ... we do not know whether their lack of a sense of efficacy occurs because they have an adversarial point of view or they lack skills, or because there is a cultural division.   (Keyes, 2000: 111)

Points to Ponder

- Which model of parental involvement is closer to yours? How do you think that Ingrid and Sally (in the story) would each answer this question?
- Do you think that early childhood education and care staff need to be trained in how to involve parents in their work, or is it just common sense?

Points to Discuss

- Are you equally comfortable with Model 1 and Model 2? How do you explain any difference in your feelings?
- Do you think that the staff in the Keyes (2000) study would have more success in involving parents if they adopted the approach described in the Knopf and Swick (2006) study? How do you think that Ingrid and Sally (in the story) would react if they read the Knopf and Swick (2006) study?

Further reading to deepen your understanding

Ghazvini, A. and Readdick, C. (2002) Parent-caregiver communication and quality of care in diverse child care settings. *Early Childhood Research Quarterly*, 9 (2): 207–22.

Ghazvini and Readdick (2002) examined the quality of communication between 201 parents and 49 staff from 12 childcare centres in the USA. Staff regarded staff–parent communication more positively than parents did; and staff believed that it happened more frequently than parents did. How would you explain these results? Do they match your experience?

Cooper, C. (in press) Family poverty, school-based parental involvement, and policy-focused protective factors in kindergarten. *Early Childhood Research Quarterly.*

Cooper (in press) reports on the Early Childhood Longitudinal Study – Kindergarten Cohort (19,375 children) in the USA. The study asked whether (and how) parents' involvement is related to the characteristics of the kindergarten and the family. The results were consistent with the results of prior studies: poorer parents are involved in schooling less than richer parents. This study also found that the difference in involvement was less marked in schools where teachers had higher qualifications; and that outreach programmes designed to increase parent involvement may unintentionally favour middle-class parents.

References

Cooper, C. (in press) Family poverty, school-based parental involvement, and policy-focused protective factors in kindergarten. *Early Childhood Research Quarterly.*

Ghazvini, A. and Readdick, C. (2002) Parent-caregiver communication and quality of care in diverse child care settings. *Early Childhood Research Quarterly,* 9(2): 207–22.

Keyes, C. (2000) Parent-teacher partnerships: a theoretical approach for teachers. *ED470883*: 107–19.

Knopf, H. and Swick, K. (2006) How parents feel about their child's teacher/school: implications for early childhood professionals. *Early Childhood Education Journal,* 34(4): 291–6.

Lamb-Parker, F., Piotrkowski, A., Baker, A., Kesslar-Sklar, S., Clark, B. and Peay, L. (2001) Understanding barriers to parent involvement in Head Start: a research-community partnership. *Early Childhood Research Quarterly,* 16(1): 35–51.

Rimm-Kaufman, S. and Pianta, R. (2005) Family-school communication in preschool and kindergarten in the context of a relationship-enhancing intervention. *Early Education and Development,* 16(3): 288–316.

11 She'll love the sausage sizzle!

To help you quickly grasp who's who, practitioners' names are shown in upright font and parents' names are shown in *italic* font.

Kate, the co-ordinator of the Pinnacles **Early Learning Centre**, is talking with *Glennis*, the grandparent of three-year-old Eliza who may be attending the centre. Eliza's mother Anna has asked *Glennis* to attend this pre-enrolment interview, as she cannot get away from her job at this time. *Glennis* is a former early childhood teacher. She is keen to see the centre Eliza may be attending and has been looking forward to the interview.

Kate: Hello *Glennis*, thanks for coming to this interview. My name is Kate and I'm the centre's Co-ordinator. At our pre-enrolment interviews we like to tell parents about the centre's philosophy and our approach to children. I have a copy of the centre's philosophy that you can give to Anna and some back copies of the centre's newsletter in which we tell parents about the fortnightly program. The philosophy tells parents what we think is important for young children, you know – what we believe about how children grow and learn.

Glennis: Thank you. Can you tell me more about your philosophy?

Kate: Well, we run a type of program here called a developmental program. We observe the children daily and then use the observations to plan a developmentally appropriate program for individual children.

Glennis: I'm familiar with developmental approaches to children but I'd be interested to know how you involve the parents in your work with the children. I'd like to know your philosophy on working with parents.

Kate: Well, we really value parents in this centre. As I said, we have a newsletter in which we tell parents about the program and there is a parent noticeboard where staff tell parents about what is happening in each group. I can show Anna the noticeboard when she comes with Eliza on Monday. Also, we have social events once a term that we invite parents to. We love to socialise with the parents – the evenings are such fun. Perhaps you could tell Anna about the notice board and the social evenings? I'm sure she'd like to know about them.

Glennis: Of course. I'd like to know a little more about how parents get involved with the program. I'm really interested in how Anna will be involved in Eliza's program.

Kate: Oh, I see. Well, the parents are involved strongly in our fundraising. Most of the parents really love the annual sausage sizzle. We give a prize for the parent who sells the most sausages. It becomes a real competition between the parents and we raise lots of money that way. I'm sure Anna will love that too.

Glennis: Yes, but do you talk with the parents about the program content at all? Eliza has been doing movement and dance with me for some time and she really is so excited about . . .

Kate: (cuts in) You needn't worry about that. All our staff are highly qualified and as part of their training, they each learnt about movement and dance with young children. They bring that into their program based on their understandings of each child's developmental needs and interests. By that I mean that we look at how each individual child is growing and changing over time and how that fits with their age. Do you remember I told you that we run a strong developmental program here based on our observations of the children? Well, that's what I mean by a developmental program. It suits every child and it will suit Eliza because we will look at how she is growing and changing and plan according to that.

Glennis: Yes, I do remember.

Kate: Good. Anything else for now?

Glennis: I think not. Thank you for your time. I think that's all for now.

Resources for thinking and talking about staff–parent relationships

Research Snippets

Here are two snippets from the research concerning parents' role in early childhood education and care settings. Research Snippet 1 comes from an extensive review of the literature on how to involve First Nations communities and families in schools in Canada (First Nations Education Council, 2009). While the snippet concerns a specific school, it has lessons that can be applied in a range of settings – for example, that creative approaches are needed and that a solution in one community may fail in another. (It also emphasizes that parental 'involvement' does not always and necessarily mean fundraising!) Research Snippet 2 is from a study of a kindergarten in Auckland, New Zealand where staff and parents changed parents' involvement from just helping with domestic chores to participating directly in the children's education (Billman et al., 2005).

Following each Research Snippet are some 'Points to Ponder' and some 'Points to Discuss', which may help you decide what you think about Kate's approach (in the story) to parent involvement at the Pinnacles Centre.

> **Research Snippet 1: Literature Review on Current Practices in First Nation Parents and Community Involvement (First Nations Education Council, 2009)**

Research Snippet 1 comes from one of five case studies of successful partnerships between schools and First Nations communities included in a review of the research literature on how best to involve First Nations families and communities in schools in Canada. The review was a response to findings by the First Nations Education Council that there are several barriers to First Nations parent involvement in schools and that there is tension and poor communication between schools and First Nations parents.

Some key findings

- The Eskasoni Elementary and Middle School sought diverse ways to create partnerships between parents, communities and school, because in their experience, something that works in one community may fail in another.
- The school has found that parents are uninterested in fundraising and other ancillary roles; but special workshops for parents with children with special needs have been well attended.
- The school has improved its relationship with parents through 'positive feedback'. Specifically:

Each teacher is expected to visit each of their students at home in each of their first five years of education, to get to know the family and to focus on positive experiences. In subsequent years, parents receive a positive telephone call about each of their children each term. Such 'positive feedback' has built rapport with the parents and led them to look positively on the school system.

(First Nations Education Council, 2009: 15)

Points to Ponder

- Should a teacher be expected to do 'extra-curricular' work (e.g. visiting or telephoning parents) as part of their job? How do you think that Kate (in the story) would react to such an expectation?
- Do you think that the fact that the Eskasoni Elementary/Middle School was trying to involve specific racial/ethnic communities means that its approach to building parent involvement cannot be applied elsewhere?

Points to Discuss

- Who benefits and who loses when parent involvement in early childhood education and care programmes is restricted to fundraising?
- Does the fact that *Glennis* (in the story) is 'familiar with developmental approaches to children' mean that she is more likely to respond to the Eskasoni Elementary and Middle School School approach than other family members?

Research Snippet 2: Teacher-parent partnerships: sharing understandings and making changes (Billman et al., 2005)

This small-scale qualitative study was undertaken at a time of increasing emphasis on partnerships in early childhood education and care settings in New Zealand. The study explored how three teachers and eight mothers changed their views on parents' roles in a kindergarten programme over time. The researchers collected data using field notes of observations and conversations with staff; and they interviewed the parents and teachers in separate focus groups.

Some key findings

- Parents said that their involvement in the Centre consisted mainly of helping with domestic chores (e.g. preparing food and tidying the centre). Staff said that they were concerned at parents' lack of time to be involved in other activities, but also that some parents were more comfortable doing domestic chores.
- When the researcher revealed the contrast in parents' and staff's views, staff sought to change parents' involvement by changing the snack time routine and by employing a teacher aid. Staff and parents began an action research project that aimed to shift parents' roles away from domestic chores and towards direct involvement in the children's education. For example:

Teachers . . . developed an emergent curriculum notice board so that parents could see what was currently the focus in the kindergarten programme. This was placed prominently in the kindergarten and used large photographs to attract parents' attention. It encouraged parents to share their expertise, resources and experiences to support children's learning. . . . In addition, the teachers developed a "Question Board" where children's questions were displayed. Parents were encouraged to bring in information on these topics. Some parents also added questions that their children asked at home.   (Billman et al., 2005: 47)

Points to Ponder

- How would parents in an early childhood education and care setting that you know describe their role? How would the staff describe the parents' role?
- Do you think that Kate (in the story) would feel at home with the approach to parent involvement in Billman et al's (2005) research?

> **Points to Discuss**
>
> - Who benefits and who loses when parent involvement in early childhood education and care programmes is restricted to domestic chores and tidying up?
> - What differences do you see between the approach to parent involvement at Eskasoni Elementary and Middle School, at the centre in Billman et al.'s (2005) research and at the Pinnacles Early Learning Centre (in the story)? How do you think such differences in approach emerge?

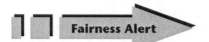

Fairness Alert

As we have seen in the story and in the research, many early childhood staff regard themselves as qualified experts doing their job and believe that parents place their children in their care because of their expertise. These staff believe that parents' involvement in the life of a centre – while important – should reflect their lack of professional expertise and so should be restricted to relatively mundane tasks, such as raising funds or doing domestic chores. These beliefs, however well intentioned, are examples of an unfair thinking habit called 'privileging' – seeing yourself and/or your group as more important than anyone else. Specifically, in this instance we present how what is considered 'expert' knowledge can be privileged:

- Privileging staff's professional expertise concerning children in general over parents' knowledge and opinions concerning their specific children.

Here is an example of privileging from the story:

Glennis: Yes, but do you talk with the parents about the program content at all? Eliza has been doing movement and dance with me for some time and she really is so excited about . . .

Kate: (cuts in) You needn't worry about that. All our staff are highly qualified and as part of their training, they each learnt about movement and dance with young children. . . . Do you remember I told you that we run a strong developmental program here based on our observations of the children? Well, that's what I mean by a developmental program. It suits every child and it will suit Eliza because we will look at how she is growing and changing and plan according to that.

The example of privileging we have taken from the research literature is from a small-scale New Zealand study that highlights the mismatch between parents' and teachers' perspectives about the role of parents who help in the kindergarten (Billman et al., 2005). The quote we have used is from a transcript of field notes taken by a researcher.

> Anne offers to stay to (provide) parent help today as Nicola had put a message on the (kindergarten) notice board asking if anyone could stay. At one stage, Anne stands behind and talks to the group of children investigating the arrival of a block of clay with Nicola. She asks open questions. However, perhaps as she is not seated with them, or perhaps because they don't know her so well or aren't used to parents being involved in play, the children do not respond to her. . . . Towards the end of the session, Julie asks Anne to fold the newsletters and put them in the pockets for parents to collect at the end of the session. Anne immediately agrees to do so. (Has she retreated to the safety of the domestic tasks?)
>
> (Billman et al., 2005: 46)

Why privileging is unfair

- It dismisses the skills and knowledge that parents can offer in early childhood education and care settings, making parents feel like 'second-class citizens'.
- It assumes that professional knowledge about children in general is always better than parents' anecdotal knowledge about their specific children.
- It implies that parents do not really know what is best for their children.
- It assumes that professionals will always have 'the right answer', but professional knowledge changes over time, so 'the right answer' can be different at different times.

How you can counter privileging

- Assume that parents have interesting views, ideas, skills and knowledge that could enhance a programme.

- Be alert to anything that implies that parents can only be domestic helpers in early childhood education and care programmes.
- Do not assume that people will always defer to 'the expert'.
- Do not assume that professional knowledge about children in general is always better than parents' detailed knowledge about their specific children.
- Regard differences in opinions (e.g. about young children's care and education) as normal and desirable.
- Actively encourage parents to give their views about their children's education and care, especially if they are reluctant; and show that their views can make a difference.
- Be prepared to learn about the specific ways in which each family thinks about their children.
- Assume that parents and staff have equal rights to hold and express ideas about how children learn.
- Regard parents' knowledge as supplementary (not subordinate) to professional knowledge and vice versa.
- Encourage parents to share their knowledge of children with each other to find commonalities, differences and links with professional knowledge.

Points to Ponder

- How could Kate (in the story) have maintained her status as a professional without privileging her professional knowledge?
- How could *Glennis* (in the story) have countered the privileging of Kate's professional knowledge? Could *Anna* do the same when (if?) she visits the Pinnacles Early Learning Centre?

Points to Discuss

- Who benefits and who loses when parent involvement in an early childhood education and care programme is restricted to mundane tasks?
- Are parents more likely than staff to criticize privileging and want to counter it?

Models of staff–parent relationships around parents' involvement in programmes

Privileging professional knowledge can be an attractive option to some staff, while some parents would assume that they should defer to professional knowledge. On the other hand, the early childhood literature is full of assurances that parent involvement is good for everyone involved. Below are two models that summarize these conflicting approaches to parents' involvement in early childhood education and care programmes. Each model underpins advice to early childhood education and care staff in the *Early Childhood Education Journal*. Model 1 underpins two articles that draw on the research literature on parent involvement in early childhood education and care settings to advise staff on how best to manage that involvement. Model 2 underpins an editorial that examines how early childhood education and care environments can promote teachers' professional development. The models are followed by some 'Points to Ponder' and some 'Points to Discuss', which may help you decide what you think about how the Pinnacles (in the story) involves parents in its programme.

Model 1: Parents' contributions are just add-ons

Sometimes in early childhood classrooms we inform parents that we want them to be involved in the process of providing care and education to their children, but don't have an identified need for assistance. So when parents arrive at the classroom or school to help, we feel compelled to give them something to do, to make them feel like they are contributing, but often delegate unimportant tasks. This is likely to convey to parents that their assistance in the classroom is not really helpful, that we do not think that they are capable of really contributing meaningfully to the classroom, or that we are not organized enough to use their help effectively.

(Knopf and Swick, 2006: 295)

- Bring families into the classroom.
- Request that parents complete a wide-ranging checklist of ways they would like to be involved. Match parental availability and interests to classroom needs. This can raise family members' awareness of the many possible forms of participation.
- Develop "job descriptions" to clarify what you need from classroom and at-home volunteers. Clear communication and encouragements will be appreciated, and will ensure that you get the kind of help you need. (Carlisle et al., 2005: 159)

Model 2: Parents' contributions are essential

On-going communication between parents and teachers supports teacher growth as they rethink their practices in response to parent concerns and questions. It was because of parent observations about their children that we studied and learned about Autism and Aspberger's Syndrome, American Sign Language, applied behavior analysis, and re-thought scheduling to meet the needs of more active children. Similarly, when parents and other care-giving adults are invited to share their talents and interests in classroom activities, teacher content knowledge expands and the curriculum becomes richer and more authentic. We learned about bones, identifying herbivores and carnivores, and how to hatch butterflies and chickens from several parent biologists. We just finished a year teaching children poetry with a parent-poet, and implemented writing workshops with assistance from a parent who trained at Columbia Teachers College with Lucy Calkins (1994).

(Jaruszewicz and White, 2009: 172)

Points to Ponder

- Which model of parents' involvement in programmes is closer to yours?
- Which model would Kate (in the story) say is closer to her approach? What did she say in the story that led you to think this?

Points to Discuss

- Do you think that teachers' and parents' contributions are equally important to the success of an early childhood education and care programme?
- If the *Early Childhood Education Journal* invited *Glennis* (in the story) to submit an article on building positive staff–parent relationships, what do you think she might write about? What did she say in the story that led you to think this?

Further reading to deepen your understanding

Zellman, G. and Perlman, M. (2006) Parent involvement in child care settings: conceptual and measurement issues. *Early Child Development and Care*, 176(5): 521–38.

As part of a larger USA study of parent involvement, Zellman and Perlman (2006) reviewed five instruments that researchers use to measure parent involvement: the Parent Child Care Involvement (PCCI) measure; the National Association for the Education of Young Children (NAEYC) measure of parent involvement; the National Longitudinal Survey of Youth (NLSY) questions about parent–provider contact; the Family–Provider Partnership (FPP) measure; and the items about parent involvement in the Early Childhood Environment Rating Scale – Revised (ECERS-R). The article shows the strengths and weaknesses of each instrument and, as such, it can help you to cast a critical eye over research reports from the USA on parent involvement. How do you think that *Glennis* (in the story) would measure parent involvement?

Keyes, C. (2000) Parent–teacher partnerships: a theoretical approach for teachers. *ED470883*: 107–19.

Keyes (2000) provides a very clear and succinct overview of different ways to think about parent–teacher relationships. As you read this article, ask yourself how *Glennis* and Kate (in the story) would each respond to each model.

References

Billman, N., Geddes, C. and Hedges, H. (2005) Teacher–parent partnerships: sharing understandings and making changes. *Australian Journal of Early Childhood*, 30(1): 44–9.

Carlisle, E., Stanley, L. and Kemple, K. (2005) Opening doors: understanding school and family influences on family involvement. *Early Childhood Education Journal*, 33(3): 155–62.

First Nations Education Council (2009) *Literature Review on Current Practices in First Nation Parents and Community Involvement*. Canada: First Nations Education Council.

Jaruszewicz, C. and White, M. (2009) The teachergarten: creating an environment conducive to meaningful teacher growth. *Early Childhood Education Journal*, 37(3): 171–4.

Keyes, C. (2000) Parent-teacher partnerships: a theoretical approach for teachers. *ED470883*: 107–19.

Knopf, H. and Swick, K. (2006) How parents feel about their child's teacher/ school: implications for early childhood professionals. *Early Childhood Education Journal*, 34(4): 291–6.

Zellman, G. and Perlman, M. (2006) Parent involvement in child care settings: conceptual and measurement issues. *Early Child Development and Care*, 176(5): 521–38.

12 I'm learning how to teach my child to read

The story

To help you quickly grasp who's who, practitioners' names are shown in upright font and parents' names are shown in *italic* font.

In Vanessa's early childhood classroom, it is 'Literacy Hour'. Vanessa has set the children to work in groups; she is working with a group of children who are practising writing. *Pam* is a parent of one of the children and she helps Vanessa occasionally around literacy. Today, *Pam* has read a story to a group of children and is about to begin reading another one. Su Jing is an early literacy adviser from the Department of Education who is visiting the classroom and Vanessa invites *Pam* to describe her involvement in early literacy to Su Jing.

> Vanessa: Su Jing is interested in our early reading program. I've told her that we think that co-operation between the home and the kindergarten is important for literacy and that we think that parents can play a really valuable role by supporting their children's literacy and by creating a good background for children's literacy to develop. Now, it would be good for *her* to hear a parent's perspective on the program.
>
> Su Jing: Hello, *Pam*. What have you been doing today around literacy?
>
> *Pam:* Well, I've been reading today's focus story to the more advanced readers in the group.
>
> Su Jing: How often do you do that?
>
> *Pam:* As often as possible. We are encouraged to help once a fortnight, but I work part-time so it's hard to manage that. I try, however, because I'm learning lots about how to teach Jane – my younger child – to read and I don't want people to think that I don't care about her literacy. She's been struggling and I think this will help me

to help her. Vanessa thinks that it's really important for me to attend. I think I've been going about it the wrong way at home. I've been reading Jane stories that are too advanced for her at present. She likes them, but I don't think it helps her focus on the words on the page enough. She listens to the stories but doesn't focus on the words.

Su Jing: Surely, it's important that Jane enjoys the stories?

Pam: Yes, but I also think I need to learn more about how to help her with specific text recognition skills if she is to improve her reading at school. I learn how to do that here. I really didn't understand much about early literacy development before the program. I just loved reading Jane stories. I still read to her lots, but I know now that I need to get better at understanding her developmental stage and targeting my reading to that. I think I did it all wrong with Karen – my older child. I want to get it right this time, but it's hard when you know your child loves the wrong stories. I'm really torn at times about what to do for the best.

(Vanessa leaves the classroom)

Su Jing: Can you talk with Vanessa about your dilemmas?

Pam: Not really, I don't want her to think that I haven't understood what she's telling me. I do understand, but Jane loves all sorts of stories and we have more fun with the stories when I'm not focusing on her reading skills. I'm not ignorant or neglectful about her reading skills, I'm just not sure where fun fits into it all.

Su Jing: Has Vanessa suggested what you might do about reading at home?

Pam: Not really. I think that she prefers to me to pick up ideas while I'm helping her in the classroom. She has her ways of doing things, I suppose.

(Vanessa re-enters the classroom and *Pam* returns to her group)

Vanessa: Did you and *Pam* have a good chat?

Su Jing: Yes, it was helpful. Tell me, do parents get involved in teaching literacy from the start?

Vanessa: No. We're in a bit of a disadvantaged area here, as I expect you noticed, so we can't expect the families to be able to do much more than provide that background, as I said. And to be honest, I don't think that many of them do that very well – they don't do specific things like going to the library or reading books with their children. And anyway, it's part of our job here to teach literacy here – it's part of what we do – so we get them to help in that way. Even then, they can sometimes get a bit too involved and can't keep a professional distance.

Su Jing: But *Pam* says that she's reading quite a lot to her daughter and that she read to her older child, too. She seems keen to do her best for her children.

Resources for thinking and talking about staff–parent relationships

Research Snippets

Here are two snippets from the extensive research about young children and literacy. Research Snippet 1 is taken from a Jordanian study which contrasts parents' and staff's views on parents' role in teaching literacy (Al-Momania et al., 2008). It includes some very strong statements by parents that they feel alienated from their children's literacy teaching. There are some resonances here with the discussion (in the story) between Su Jing and Vanessa about parents' role in teaching literacy. Research Snippet 2 is from a study that evaluated studies of parent involvement (Mattingly et al., 2002). It highlights the very different ways in which researchers, parents and staff can understand parent involvement and, therefore, the need to scrutinize carefully any claims about whether and how to involve parents in their children's education.

Following each Research Snippet are some 'Points to Ponder' and some 'Points to Discuss', which may help you decide what you think about how Vanessa (in the story) assessed *Pam's* capacity to teach literacy.

Research Snippet 1: Teaching reading in the early years: exploring home and kindergarten relationships (Al-Momania et al., 2008)

Al-Momania et al. (2008) asked 40 parents and 20 teachers in Jordan about parents' involvement in teaching four- and five-year-old children to read.

Some key findings

The teachers

- Most teachers believed that kindergarten–home co-operation was important, but parental interest could be excessive, parents could be unco-operative and home may not be an appropriate place for formal literacy development (Al-Momania et al., 2008: 8).
- Some teachers believed that parents' role is to provide a background for and support of literacy development, but most teachers do not encourage parents to provide direct literacy instruction (Al-Momania et al., 2008: 10).

The parents

- Most parents did not perceive opportunities for involvement or support for at-home literacy activities (Al-Momania et al., 2008: 11).
- Most (27/40) parents did not attend parent meetings because they did not find them helpful and several found them a waste of time. Of parent–teacher meetings one parent said:

These meetings are absolutely useless because the kindergartens do not want to involve us in the learning and teaching process. As a parent, I cannot interfere with the kindergarten's system and force it to involve us by saying to the teachers to do this or do not do that. (Al-Momania et al., 2008: 12)

Points to Ponder

- Most teachers believed that kindergarten–home co-operation was important, but several parents found parent meetings a waste of time. How do you think this conflict arose?
- Can you see the potential for similar conflict to arise between Vanessa (in the story) and parents at her kindergarten? Does anything that Vanessa said support your view?

Points to Discuss

- Did the teachers regard themselves as literacy experts, as collaborators with parents, as partners with parents or as uncertain?
- Who knows best about how to teach children to read? Why do you think this? Who (in the story) would agree with you – *Pam*, Su Jing or Vanessa?

Research Snippet 2: Evaluating evaluations: the case of parent involvement programmes (Mattingly et al., 2002)

Mattingly et al. (2002) examined 41 published reports of research on parent involvement programmes in kindergarten to year 12 in the USA. In each one, they evaluated the research design, the research data, the approach to analysis and the rigour of the conclusions. This Research Snippet consists of their conclusions and two particular concerns about the research – overgeneralization and confusion between 'association' and 'cause'.

Some key findings

(T)here was, 'little empirical support for the widespread claim that parent involvement programs are an effective means of improving student achievement or changing parent, teacher, and student behaviour. We do not conclude that programs are ineffective. Rather, serious design, methodological, and analytical flaws inherent in studies evaluating the effectiveness of parent involvement programs must be addressed before definite conclusions about program effectiveness can be reached.'   (Mattingly et al., 2002: 549)

Whilst the majority of programs were located in schools with large low-income and non-White populations, they failed to take into account that within such schools there are many effective parents, strong families, and academically successful children.
(Mattingly et al., 2002: 571)

The belief that student academic success can be improved through programs designed to increase parent involvement in education is widespread in both academic and policy-making arenas. The most consistent support for such claims comes from studies demonstrating systematic covariation between parent involvement and student achievement. This article shows, however, that there is not substantial evidence to indicate a causal relationship . . .
(Mattingly et al., 2002: 572)

Points to Ponder

- Why do you think that most of the parent involvement programmes were conducted in schools with large low-income and non-white populations? How do you think that Vanessa (in the story) would answer this question?
- Should parents in poor families receive more encouragement to be involved in their children's education than parents in rich families? How did you reach your conclusion?

Points to Discuss

- What is the difference between 'systematic covariation' and 'a causal relationship'? Why and to whom does this difference matter?
- How could you discover whether parent involvement *causes* improved academic success in children, as distinct from just being associated with it?

Fairness Alerts

The story and the research literature around parent involvement include several examples of two unfair thinking habits – 'homogenizing' and 'othering'.

'Homogenizing' eradicates differences between members of gender, class, ethnic and cultural groups by assuming they do not exist. Here we are referring to a specific instance of homogenizing:

- Homogenizing individuals, families and groups in the same class.

Here is an example of homogenizing from the story:

> Vanessa: We're in a bit of a disadvantaged area here, as I expect you noticed, so we can't expect the families to be able to do much more than provide that background, as I said.

Here is an example of homogenizing from the research. It comes from a report about a family literacy programme in Canada involving 12 teachers and 108 children in their first grade of primary school (Saint-Laurent and Giasson, 2005).

> While children from middle **socio-economic status** (**SES**) families are familiar with storybook reading when they begin school, those from low SES families tend to be disadvantaged in literacy development because book reading experiences are sparse.
>
> (Saint-Laurent and Giasson, 2005: 255)

Why homogenizing is unfair

- People from any class are complex individuals. They will not necessarily share experiences (e.g. of early book reading), despite their common class background.
- People in each class (including you) will have had different experiences of early book reading.
- While researchers might find broad trends (e.g. around early book reading) in a class, not every individual in that class will conform to those broad trends.

How you can counter homogenizing

- Assume that people from the same class will have diverse attitudes to reading and to their children's literacy.
- Learn about the specific ways in which each family approaches reading with their child/ren and the place of storybooks in this work.
- Challenge statements that homogenize people by highlighting differences between them.

Points to Ponder

- To which gender, class, ethnic or cultural groups did/does your extended family belong? Has this influenced your attitude to literacy? Is this true for other members in your extended family or for other people in your neighbourhood?
- Have you heard people from particular gender, class, ethnic or cultural groups being 'homogenized'? Have you experienced homogenization yourself?

Points to Discuss

- When you were a young child, did you have easy access to books? Did this influence your success at reading?
- How could Su Jing (in the story) have countered Vanessa's homogenization of local people?

The second unfair thinking habit in the story and the research literature around parent involvement is 'othering' – seeing yourself and/or your group as the norm, from which everyone else deviates. Here we are referring to a specific instance of othering:

- Othering people who do not promote literacy as you do.

Here is an example of othering from the story:

> Vanessa: . . . I don't think that many of (the families) do that very well – they don't do specific things like going to the library or reading books with their children. And anyway, it's part of our job here to teach literacy here – it's part of what we do – so we get them to help in that way. Even then, they can sometimes get a bit too involved and can't keep a professional distance.

Here is an example of othering from the research. It consists of excerpts from a *Parent Child Checklist* (Stegelin, 2003) in a monograph advising early childhood education and care student teachers in the USA how to involve families in their children's literacy. In itself, it does not other anyone – but it certainly implies that parents or carers *should* do these sorts of activities and if they do not . . .

> Do you visit the library on a weekly or regular basis and make this a family event?
> Do you model a love of reading by reading a newspaper daily and subscribe to magazines for yourself?
> Do you invite your child to make shopping lists with you?
> Do you visit local museums and libraries and then discuss what you saw?
> Do you keep a family journal during vacations and then add photos to document your shared activities?
> Do you visit aging relatives in nursing homes or assisted living centers and record histories of their earlier experiences?
>
> (Stegelin, 2003: 20)

Why othering is unfair

- It promotes particular actions (e.g. reading newspapers, visiting libraries and museums, reading books with children, keeping family journals or recording aging relatives' experiences) as the right way to support young children's literacy and implies that parents or carers who do not pursue these activities do not care about their children's literacy.
- It implies that certain forms of reading (books, newspapers, journals) and sites of reading (libraries, museums) promote literacy better than others, yet offers no evidence that this is so.

How you can counter othering

- Do not assume that everyone can do all the recommended activities to support their children's literacy.
- Welcome differences in how families spend time, what they read, when they read it, how they shop and what they do at the weekend.
- Accept that it may be as normal and desirable to read children CD covers, political pamphlets and adverts as it is to read them newspapers and storybooks.
- Accept that it is normal to just 'enjoy the moment' on holidays, rather than always looking for 'teachable moments'.
- Consider changing your attitude to literacy if it hurts, silences or offends people with whom you are working.
- Challenging statements that 'other' people who do not support their children's literacy in recommended ways.

Points to Ponder

- Have you experienced othering (of yourself or of someone else) because of ignorance about (for example) children's literacy?
- How many of the activities recommended in the story and the research to promote children's literacy did you do as a child? What about other members of your extended family or other people in your neighbourhood?

Points to Discuss

- Do you think that there is any special value in reading storybooks (rather than other forms of reading) to children to support their literacy? How do you think that *Pam* (in the story) would answer this question?
- Are text messages on mobile phones a good resource for young children's literacy? What about emails?

Models of staff–parent relationships around children's literacy

The extensive research literature around young children's literacy includes many different models of staff–parent relationships. Model 1 underpins the study by Saint-Laurent and Giasson (2005) of a family literacy programme in Canada, which we have mentioned already. Its focus on the primacy of the teacher's role recalls Vanessa's position (in the story). Model 2 emerges from Cairney's (2000) analysis of how to create staff-parent relationships that can support young children's literacy.

Each model is followed by some 'Points to Ponder' and some 'Points to Discuss', which may help you decide what you think about the relationship that Vanessa and *Pam* (in the story) have created around children's literacy.

Model 1: Parents need teachers to tell them how to support their children's literacy

> The aim of this study was to assess the impact of a family literacy program for first graders that focused on gradually changing parental support according to the evolution of children's reading skills during the school year, and combining reading and writing activities as well as enjoyable home activities that complement the in-class teaching.
> (Saint-Laurent and Giasson, 2005: 254)

Model 2: Teachers can learn from parents how to support young children's literacy

> The relationship between school success and home factors has been confirmed, but there is much to be learned about how schools can be more responsive to cultural diversity and the uneven spread of resources within and across communities.

> The big challenge is to transform schools into sites for learning that are far more responsive to the social and cultural diversity of the communities that they serve.   (Cairney, 2000: 172)

We would suggest the Ministry look at ways of encouraging teachers to learn from parents about children's home-literacy experiences and practices, and reflect on ways of adapting their literacy programmes to take cognizance of this. This aspect is what makes this home–school partnership programme so different from many others – the key difference being that it is intended to build on the strengths of what the child brings to school in terms of literacy experiences. If this is the part that is missing in practice, it pulls the programme down to other similar, 'transmission-type' programmes where schools are telling parents what they think should be happening at home. (Brooking, 2007: 158)

Points to Ponder

- Which of those two models of staff–parent relationships around children's literacy is closer to your own? Which is closer to Vanessa's approach (in the story)?
- In an early childhood education and care setting that you know, does the literacy programme acknowledge and include children's experiences of literacy at home? What do you see as the advantages and disadvantages of doing so?

Points to Discuss

- Is literacy a set of skills that are universal, or does literacy vary between cultures and languages? What roles do teachers have in each case?
- Are parents/carers a child's first teachers of literacy?

Further reading to deepen your thinking and talking

Cairney, T.H. (2002) Bridging home and school literacy: in search of transformative approaches to curriculum. *Early Child Development and Care*, 172: 153–73.

Cairney (2002) highlights the different definitions/understandings of literacy and shows that our choice of definition/understanding influences our view of parents' and teachers' role in children's literacy. How do you think that *Pam* and Vanessa (in the story) might each respond to this article?

Cairney, T. (2000) Beyond the classroom walls: the rediscovery of the family and community as partners in education. *Educational Review*, 52: 163–74.

Cairney (2000) rejects 'deficit' views of families and communities that say they are inadequate teachers of children's literacy and calls for partnerships between parents and schools that reflect and draw on ethnic and linguistic diversity. Do you think that Vanessa (in the story) believes that literacy is a universal set of skills and, if so, how do you think she would respond to this article?

References

Al-Momania, I., Ihmeidehb, F. and Abu Naba'h, A. (2008) Teaching reading in the early years: exploring home and kindergarten relationships. *Early Child Development and Care*, 180(6): 1–18.

Brooking, K. A. R., J. (2007) *Evaluation of the Home–school Partnership: Literacy Programme*. Report for NZCER, for the Ministry of Education.

Cairney, T. (2000) Beyond the classroom walls: the rediscovery of the family and community as partners in education. *Educational Review*, 52(2): 163–74.

Cairney, T.H. (2002) Bridging home and school literacy: in search of transformative approaches to curriculum. *Early Child Development and Care*, 172(2): 153–73.

Mattingly, D., Prislin, R., Mckenzie, T., Rodriguez, J. and Kayzar, B. (2002) Evaluating the evaluations: the case of parent involvement programs. *Review of Educational Research*, 72(4): 549–76.

Saint-Laurent, L. and Giasson, J. (2005) Effects of a family literacy program adapting parental intervention to first graders' evolution of reading and writing abilities. *Journal of Early Childhood Literacy*, 5(3): 253–78.

Stegelin, D.A. (2003) *Family Literacy Strategies: First Steps to Academic Success*. Clemson, SC: National Dropout Prevention Center.

13 They're just not involved

To help you quickly grasp who's who, practitioners' names are shown in upright font and parents' names are shown in *italic* font.

Jennifer, Aysha and Barbara are attending a professional development day. They have not met before, but have just come out of a session about parent–staff relationships and are chatting over morning coffee.

Jennifer: The trouble is, the parents at my centre don't seem interested in what goes on there and they don't seem to read any of the documentation that we prepare about the children and the program. I want to include parents' voices in the curriculum in respectful ways that mean something to them, but ... there's never enough time in my day to consult them all – and not really anywhere to do it.

Aysha: It can be really hard to find out what parents think. I ended up using a short questionnaire to discover what parents of the children in my room thought of my program. Only a few of them knew about the program, but most wanted to be involved – and in different ways, ranging from 'conversations with staff' to 'commenting on the program in writing'.

Barbara: I asked a couple of parents at my centre why they didn't get involved more and they said that it was because they didn't know how to!

Jennifer: What did the parents in your survey say about why they weren't involved already?

Aysha: There were lots of reasons and I must say I hadn't really thought about some of them. Some parents said that they couldn't get involved because they didn't have the time after work. Others said that they wanted to be involved only if their child became unhappy or wasn't developing properly. And others just didn't want to be involved at all.

Barbara: Yeah – I've got a few of those!

Aysha: Well, these were actually the most interesting replies – these were the ones that I hadn't thought about. Some parents said that they kept out of the program because they wanted their child to be in a completely different environment to their home – including them not being part of it. Others said that they didn't really need to be involved because they got new ideas from the program and used them at home. And finally, some just said that they saw no point in getting involved because the staff are the experts, so they should leave it to us.

Jennifer: That's really interesting! So it's not that you just hadn't found the right way to involve parents . . . they had good reasons for *not* getting involved.

Aysha: That's right. And I don't think it would matter what we did – they still wouldn't get involved for the same reasons. We expect parents to get involved with the program, but parents are busy people and we must remember that.

Jennifer: So in my own case, rather than trying to dream up new ways to get through to parents – and then getting fed up when they don't – I should try to find out how they see their relationship with the Centre and then work with them on that basis. Hmmm.

Barbara: That's all very well, but don't forget that we *have* to involve parents – it's in the accreditation rules.

Aysha: Of course, you're right, but I think that I've been thinking, '*This* is how a good parent behaves, so what's *wrong* with these people?!' But that's about involving them just on my terms. So, in fact, I've been the problem, not them.

Resources for thinking and talking about staff–parent relationships

Research Snippets

Here are two snippets from the research about how parents and teachers negotiate their perceptions of each other. Research Snippet 1 is from a late 1990s study in the USA (Izzo et al., 1999) that raises a question about parent involvement that, even after two decades and despite its significance of policy and practice, very few people ask: is more parent involvement necessarily better for children? Research Snippet 2 is from a study in Canada in which

French-Canadian parents whose child had been violent discussed their attitudes to being involved in their child's education (Drolet et al., 2007). It, too, questions assumptions: can parent involvement be driven by negative factors, rather than the positive ones that everyone assumes?

Following each Research Snippet are some 'Points to Ponder' and some 'Points to Discuss', which may help you decide what you think influences parent involvement and how best to decide how a 'good parent' (Aysha, in the story) behaves.

> ### Snippet 1: A longitudinal assessment of teacher perceptions of parent involvement in children's education and school performance (Izzo et al., 1999)

This three-year longitudinal urban study of how parent involvement relates to children's performance in USA schools tracked 1,205 children moving from kindergarten through to grade 3 and their teachers. Researchers analysed teacher reports of the quantity and quality of parents' involvement in their children's educational activities at school and at home.

> ### Some key findings
>
> (T)he sheer quantity of parent–teacher interactions predicts that children's classroom behavior will actually worsen over time. It is likely that this negative association exists not because parent–teacher contact leads children to behave poorly, but because, with other positive aspects of parent involvement controlled for (for example, attending school activities, positive interactions with the teacher), those contacts are primarily associated with a child's existing behavior problems. In fact, Leitch and Tangri (1988) found that children's behavior problems were among the most frequent reasons for parent–teacher contacts. Interestingly, number of contacts showed a strong positive correlation with quality of parent–teacher interactions, which suggests that even though greater contact doesn't necessarily relate to better performance, it does relate to teacher perceptions of constructive parent–teacher interactions. Overall, these findings suggest that it will be worthwhile for schools to put effort into fostering more constructive interactions between parents and teachers, instead of focusing solely on the number of contacts.   (Izzo et al., 1999: 835)

Points to Ponder

- In your experience, is the frequency of contact between staff and parents linked to a child's performance in early childhood education and care settings?
- Do you believe that the more often staff and parents meet the better it is for all concerned?

Points to Discuss

- If Izzo et al. (1999) conducted a similar study at the centre where Barbara (in the story) works, do you think that the results would be similar or different?
- In your experience, are parents who get involved in their children's education and care likely to be (a) satisfied or (b) dissatisfied with the quality of that education and care?

Snippet 2: Strengths-based approach and coping strategies used by parents whose young children exhibit violent behaviour: collaboration between schools and parents (Drolet et al., 2007)

Drolet et al. (2007) used qualitative structured and unstructured telephone interviews to talk with 60 French-speaking Canadian parents of children between 3 and 9 years of age who were behaving violently in school settings. The researchers were interested in how these parents negotiated their relationships with schools.

Some key findings

- Parents developed various relationships with the school, from working with the school to solve problems to resisting or rebelling against the school's suggestions. More specifically:

  The first step taken by one-third of the parents (21/60) to influence their child's school situation entailed making contact with the school. Their aim was either to discuss a particular problem caused by their child's violent conduct, or to follow it up. If there had been a lack of communication with the school, the parents wanted to be aware of all the details related to the difficulties encountered by their child and to understand how the teacher or the principal proceeded to manage the problem.   (Drolet et al., 2007: 445)

For one-third (20/60) of the respondents, direct opposition to the school appeared to be a major strategy in their attempt to influence the school's decisions concerning their children. These parents took pains to assert themselves so that the interventions targeting their children were, to their eyes, more appropriate. As stated, these parents clearly and firmly resisted the use of Ritalin or other coercive measures proposed by the school. Some of the respondents reacted especially against the unilateral nature of those disciplinary measures which, according to them, the school justified too much as legitimate or legal prerogatives. Other parents claimed that, despite their efforts to cooperate, they ran up against institutional barriers: "The principal refuses to set up a mentoring system in the schoolyard for my son in kindergarten; a kid in Grade 6 could easily look after him. That's not the way the principal does things! She's not at all interested in changing her routine."   (Drolet et al., 2007: 447)

Points to Ponder

- What experience do you have of parents resisting staff in early childhood education and care settings? How do you think that Barbara and Aysa (in the story) would each react to resistant parents?
- Do you see any links between the findings of the two research projects – Drolet et al. (2007) and Izzo et al. (1999)?

Points to Discuss

- Is parent resistance a form of parent involvement?
- In your experience, do early childhood education and care settings regard all forms of parent involvement in the same way?
- How could you use the study by Drolet et al. (2007) to explore the topic of parent involvement at a professional development day for early childhood education and care staff?

Fairness Alert

Groups of staff and groups of parents are as likely as anyone else to have differences of opinion or perspective. However, parents sometimes see the staff at their children's centre as a coherent group, whose members will always react in the same way; and staff sometimes see parents in the same way. This can lead individuals – whether staff or parents – to make assumptions about 'them' and can make them wary of raising a particular issue, for fear of how 'they' will react. Such behaviour is an example of an unfair thinking habit called 'homogenizing' – eradicating differences by assuming they do not exist. Here we emphasize how expectations can homogenize, specifically:

- Homogenizing parents who do not meet expectations of 'good' parents.

Here is an example of homogenizing from the story:

Jennifer: So in my own case, rather than trying to dream up new ways to get through to parents – and then getting fed up when they don't – I should try to find out how they see their relationship with the Centre and then work with them on that basis. Hmmm.

Barbara: That's all very well, but don't forget that we *have* to involve parents – it's in the accreditation rules.

Aysha: Of course, you're right, but I think that I've been thinking, 'This is how a good parent behaves, so what's *wrong* with these people?!' But that's about involving them just on my terms. So, in fact, I've been the problem, not them.

An example of homogenizing from the research is taken from an article in which Latino immigrant parents in California (USA) shared their experiences of attempting to become involved in their children's education (Fred Ramirez, 2003). The first quote includes a statement by one of the immigrant Mexican parents about what makes it difficult for him to be a parent who participates. The second quote highlights how the teachers positioned some parents as 'bad' parents.

> The parents seemed to feel there was an expectation of them as parents with which many felt uncomfortable. Armando from Mexico shared: "I have to work at night, and teachers are telling me I have to come to a gathering at the school at night. I can't do both."
>
> (Fred Ramirez, 2003: 100)

> The teacher then responded: "The parents need to turn off the TVs and take care of their kids." The parents felt the teacher believed that they, as parents, did not care about their children. This was apparent when parents heard teachers mention that, if parents did not show up to the Open House, "They didn't care about their kids." This upset many of the parents during the interviews because many, as stated above, never heard of the Open House or had other difficulties attending the Open House.   (Fred Ramirez, 2003: 101)

Why homogenizing is unfair

- Assuming that all parents have unlimited time to attend events at the centre ignores particular parents' particular demands on their time (e.g. family duties, work requirements).
- Criticizing all parents in a particular social or cultural group for particular behaviours (e.g. how long their children watch television; failing to attend parents' meetings) implies that they behave like that because they belong to that group, rather than because of their individual circumstances.
- People from any social or cultural group are complex individuals who, despite their shared background, will not *necessarily* share experiences of education.
- Researchers may find broad trends (e.g. attitudes to education) in a particular social or cultural group, but not every individual in that group will conform to those broad trends.

How you can counter homogenizing

- Ask parents when and for how long they can attend events at the centre and plan accordingly.
- Be aware that members of a particular social or cultural group may share certain beliefs and practices . . . but may differ in whether and how they apply them.
- Assume that each parent may have particular and valid reasons for being either involved or uninvolved in their child's education and care.
- Ask 'uninvolved' parents just how they see their role in their children's education; be prepared for 'unacceptable' answers . . . and be prepared to learn from them.
- Look for statements or actions that homogenize a group of people (e.g. a class, a racial group) and be prepared to challenge them.

Points to Ponder

- Have you experienced homogenizing practices or statements similar to those reported by Fred Ramirez (2003)?
- How could you use Aysha's 'most interesting replies' to her survey to help you and others to avoid homogenizing parents and to challenge the idea that there is just one way to be a 'good' parent and that is to be involved?

Points to Discuss

- In your experience, what sorts of 'uninvolved' parents are most likely to be 'homogenized'? Do you know why each sort of 'uninvolved' parents was uninvolved?
- Can you add any reasons for parents' lack of involvement to the list in the story? (Remember: they need not be negative reasons.)

Models of staff–parent relationships around parent involvement

Here are two quite different models of relationships between parents and staff, each forming a particular approach to assessing parents' involvement in early childhood education and care. Model 1 underpinned US kindergarten teachers' use of a formal Teacher Involvement Measure (Rimm-Kaufman et al., 2003). Model 2 emerges from a study of whether and how parents participated actively in a programme within the **Sure Start** initiative in the UK (Morrow and Malin, 2004). (The Sure Start social inclusion programme began in 1998. It is intended to close the gap in educational achievement between children from poor and rich families.)

The models are followed by some 'Points to Ponder' and some 'Points to discuss', which may help you decide what you think about different parents' different beliefs about 'involvement' in early childhood education and care.

Model 1: The more parent involvement, the better for everyone

Teachers completed the Parent and Teacher Involvement Measure (Conduct Problems Research Group, 1995) in April of the children's kindergarten year. This is a 21-item teacher-report measure of families' involvement in their child's education. Eleven questions measured frequency of contact. Teachers were asked, for example, "How often has this child's parents called you in the past year?" and responded "Never, once or twice a year, almost every month, almost every week, more than once per week." Ten questions asked about parents' degree of participation in their child's education. For example, teachers were asked "How much do you feel this parent has the same goals for his/her child as the school does?" or "How involved is this parent in his/her child's education and school life?" or "How important is education in this family?" Each item was rated on a 5-point scale; higher scores indicate greater involvement.   (Rimm-Kaufman et al., 2003: 184)

Model 2: Parent involvement reflects balance of power in parent-staff relationships

Relationship power . . . is concerned with the ability to influence others and can operate at individual and group levels. As people realize their own strength and potential, they renegotiate the power relationship with professionals. Parents (or service users) may take on more of the functions that professionals traditionally perform as they feel they have a contribution to make, and may contribute more equally to decision-making. For professionals, this may involve dilemmas or conflicts and a reappraisal of their role and contribution and how their expertise fits in.   (Morrow and Malin, 2004: 173)

Points to Ponder

- Do you think that the frequency of a parent's contact with early childhood staff (as measured by the Parent and Teacher Involvement Measure) reflects their involvement in their child's education and care? How do you think Barbara and Jennifer (in the story) would each respond to this question?
- Do you think that 'relationship power' reflects parents' involvement in their child's education and care? How could you measure 'relationship power'?

Points to Discuss

- Who do you think is in the best position to assess parent involvement – parents, staff or researchers? (Or children?)
- Aysha (in the story) had concluded that, 'I'm the problem, not them (the parents).' Do you think that she's being too hard on herself? Which model is closer to her conclusion?

Further reading to deepen your understanding

Bloomquist, M., Horowitz, J., August, G., Lee, C.-Y., Realmuto, G. and Klimes-Dougan, B. (2009) Understanding parent participation in a going-to-scale implementation trial of the early risers conduct problems prevention program. *Journal of Child Family Studies*, 18(6), 710–18.

Bloomquist et al. (2009) studied a programme for parents whose children woke early and found that participation in the programme depended on several factors, including the parents' income, education and level of frustration with their child. Participation also depended on who presented the programme: the more positive and interesting the presenter, the greater the participation. While the study was not conducted in early childhood education and care settings, it is a good illustration of the many factors that can affect parent involvement in an early childhood education and care programme. Do you think that the conversation (in the story) between Jennifer, Barbara and Aysha would have been different if any of them had read this article?

Cavanagh, R. and Romanoksi, J. (2005) Parent views of involvement in their child's education: a Rasch model analysis. Paper presented at the *Annual Conference of the Australian Association for Research in Education*, Sydney.

Cavanagh and Romanoksi (2005) used a 40-item rating scale to measure Australian parents' involvement in their child's education. They asked parents to rate a number of items within three categories: the child's view of the importance of schooling, their desire to learn and their achievement and engagement; the school's focus on children, on learning and on education generally; and teachers' willingness to inform and work with parents and parents' confidence in communicating with the teacher. You could use the rating to explore what you mean by parent involvement and to reflect on how (and by whom) it might be measured. Consider how Barbara (in the story) might respond to the rating. What might Aysha (in the story) see as the pros and cons of using the rating scale?

References

Bloomquist, M., Horowitz, J., August, G., Lee, C.-Y., Realmuto, G. and Klimes-Dougan, B. (2009) Understanding parent participation in a going-to-scale implementation trial of the early risers conduct problems prevention program. *Journal of Child Family Studies*, 18(6): 710–18.

Cavanagh, R. and Romanoksi, J. (2005) Parent views of involvement in their child's education: a Rasch model analysis. Paper presented at the *Annual Conference of the Australian Association for Research in Education*, Sydney.

Drolet, M., Paquin, M. and Soutyrine, M. (2007) Strengths-based approach and coping strategies used by parents whose young children exhibit violent behaviour: collaboration between schools and parents. *Child Adolescent Social Work Journal*, 24(5): 437–53.

Fred Ramirez, A. (2003) Dismay and disappointment: parental involvement of latino immigrant parents. *Urban Review*, 35(2): 93–108.

Izzo, C., Weissberg, P., Kasprow, W. and Fendrich, M. (1999) A longitudinal assessment of teacher perceptions of parent involvement in children's education and school performance. *American Journal of Community Psychology*, 27(6): 817–39.

Morrow, G. and Malin, N. (2004) Parents and professionals working together: turning the rhetoric into reality. *Early Years*, 24(2): 163–77.

Rimm-Kaufman, S., Pianta, R., Cox, M. and Bradley, R. (2003) Teacher-rated family involvement and children's social and academic outcomes in kindergarten. *Early Education and Development*, 14(2): 179–98.

14 Boys who like to be different

To help you quickly grasp who's who, practitioners' names are shown in upright font and parents' names are shown in *italic* font.

Staff at the Gum Trees Children's Centre want to introduce a gender equity programme. They raised the idea at the last monthly staff–parents meeting and they have written about it in the centre's fortnightly newsletter. At tonight's staff–parents meeting, the proposed programme is first on the agenda. Bonnie the co-ordinator has agreed to introduce it and her colleagues Doris and Kayo are there, too. Among the parents are *Ruby*, *Tony*, *Emma* and *Rachel*.

Bonnie: The first item is our proposal for a gender equity program. We talked about this at our last meeting and there's something about it in the current newsletter. I hope everyone has had a chance to think about it. Who'd like to comment first?

Ruby: I'm really pleased that you want to deal with gender. I want my son Paul to learn that being aggressive and 'macho' isn't right – in fact, it's a problem, especially for the girls ... and for the teachers, too.

Tony: Listen. There's nothing wrong with being a proper boy and I want my son Joe to be a proper boy. I don't want him coming home from the centre all squishy and soft. If this gender equity thing means Joe's going to have to wear dresses and play with dolls, then I'm dead against it. I don't want him going gay on me!

Bonnie: *Tony*, we still don't have the final answer to how anyone develops a particular sexuality and the research shows that boys who play with dolls or wear dresses are no more or less likely to grow into gay men than any other boys. Boys play with dolls all the time – we just call them 'action figures' and 'Transformers'!

Emma: Well that may be, but I agree with *Tony.* He and I think it's important Joe really knows where he stands as a boy. I'm not really in favour of the program if it confuses him about what it means to be male. In fact, I think it's a pity that there aren't more men in childcare, so that boys who come to centres like this can have some proper role models.

Doris: But boys don't learn only from men, nor do girls learn only from women. Children observe everyone around them – men and women, boys and girls – and they can see there are various ways to be male, some more 'macho' than others. So the same boy can be 'macho' one minute and something else the next.

Rachel: I'm concerned that you don't want Joe to play with dolls, *Tony.* How else will he learn to be caring? I want my son Saul to learn to be non-sexist, gentle and caring and I don't want him getting a hard time for it. I know that Joe gives him a hard time about it, which I don't think is fair. Mind you, I want Saul to be clear he is a boy. I know what *Emma* means. I don't want him confused about his gender.

Bonnie: Of course, some ways to be a man are more widespread than others and so they're often described as 'normal' or 'traditional'. But who benefits and who loses from those dominant ways to 'be a man' and are we happy with that?

Tony: Look. I want Joe to be strong, brave and confident – just your typical boy. Anyone got a problem with that?

Kayo: Well I don't have a problem with that, *Tony,* because it applies to non-traditional boys, too. These boys must be strong, because being a boy in what to them is the 'right' way can bring them lots of challenges. They must be brave, too, to deal with other people's reactions to them. Some people think that they're odd, others just don't like them. And they must be confident, because they must continually assert that their way of being a boy is right for them, even though it's different from many others.

Rachel: I think that you're absolutely right, Kayo. Boys like my Saul can't be pushed around, *Tony.* They won't necessarily stop doing what they want to just because you tell them – they'll just do it in private.

Emma: I think that's really sad . . . in a way.

Resources for thinking and talking about staff-parent relationships

Research Snippets

Here are two snippets from the research about gender and education. Research Snippet 1 is taken from a Swedish study of what Swedish preschools call 'gender-sensitive pedagogy', which emphasizes teaching and learning for gender equity and awareness (Karlson and Simonsson, 2008). Research Snippet 2 – from an earlier study of the views and experiences of gender of children who have been raised in feminist households (Risman and Myers, 1997) – is a nice counterpoint to some early childhood education and care staff's assumption that parents are always more conservative than staff around gender issues.

Following each research snippet are some 'Points to Ponder' and some 'Points to Discuss', which may help you decide what you think about the different ways in which the adults in the story saw gender equity.

> **Research Snippet 1: Preschool work teams' view of ways of working with gender – parents' involvement (Karlson and Simonsson, 2008)**

Karlson and Simonsson (2008) used focus group interviews to explore how four preschool work teams – two from a small working class town and two from a university city – involved parents as they implemented gender-sensitive pedagogy.

Some key findings

- Staff believed that they needed to learn more about gender-sensitive pedagogy.
- Staff expected that introducing gender-sensitive pedagogy involved building partnerships with parents.
- Staff believed that parents understood 'gender-sensitive pedagogy' in diverse ways and that their role was to ensure that all parents were well-informed about it. For example:

> Teacher 2: We have tried to tell them (the parents) about our thoughts about gender and how we intend to work with that in our preschool. Then we gave some examples from our work with the children. We haven't had any resistance from the parents, such as we can hear from the other preschools.
> Teacher 1: We have met a positive response the whole time. It is a very urgent question today.
> Teacher 3: I think in our work we have met the parents in small groups and we have close discussions with them, and we don't need bigger discussions, really.
> Teacher 2: They said to us 'If you think it is good enough for our children, then we trust you.'

Interviewer: What does this closer cooperation with the parents mean?

Teacher 3: These personal contacts ... We have met the parents almost every day and have had some conversation with them, informed them what we have done during the day and what we will do next day.　　　　(Karlson and Simonsson, 2008: 174)

Points to Ponder

- Should early childhood education and care staff actively promote alternatives to traditional ways of being a boy? Who gains and who loses (a) if they do and (b) if they do not?
- Would parents of young children that you know support or resist the Swedish 'gender-sensitive pedagogy'? Would you agree with them?
- How do you think *Tony* (in the story) would respond to working in the services in this research?

Points to Discuss

- Do you think that the parents in the study were right to trust early childhood education and care staff around gender education?
- Does each of you believe that boys can learn anything from playing 'girl games', such as dolls and dressing up?
- Who from the Gum Trees Centre meeting (in the story) would be most likely to agree with you? Why do you think this?

Research Snippet 2: As the twig is bent: children reared in feminist households (Risman and Myers, 1997)

Risman and Myers (1997) collected children's stories, poems and conversations over five years to understand the experiences and attitudes of 26 children in 15 white, middle-class families in the USA that actively promoted gender equity.

Some key findings

- Parents encouraged both sons and daughters to challenge sex-role stereotypes in how they behaved and thought.
- In daily life, parents modelled non-sexist behaviors and attitudes to children.
- Children experienced considerable inconsistencies between their parents' attitudes and behaviours around gender and those of their peers, their schools and the other adults in their daily lives.
- Children believed in gender equity, but their belief was challenged regularly by their experiences outside of the family, especially in school. For instance, children 'spoke explicitly about male privilege among peers or at school' (Risman and Myers, 1997: 242).
- The children's experiences of gender in their families struggled to compete with their experiences of gender outside their families:

When family experiences collided head-on with experiences with peers, the family influences were dwarfed. For example, one 6 year old boy told us that if a magician were to turn him into a girl, he'd be different because he'd have long hair. This boy's father had a long straight black ponytail which went to the middle of his back, and his mother's hair hardly reached below her ears. A four year old boy told us that if a magician were to turn him into a girl, he'd have to do housework – despite his father's flexible work schedule, which allowed him to spend more time in domestic pursuits than his wife. Children knew that *women and men* were equal; it was *boys and girls* who were totally different. It almost seemed as if these children believed that boys and girls were opposites, but men and women magically transformed into equal and comparable people.   (Risman and Myers, 1997: 242)

The researchers concluded that:

The children in fair families have adopted their parents' egalitarian views. They believe men and women are equal, and that no jobs – inside or outside the family – ought to be sex-linked. But beyond these abstract statements concerning beliefs, these children depend on their own lived experiences for understanding gender in their childhood worlds. And they "know" that boys and girls are different – very different.   (Risman and Myers, 1997: 247)

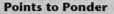

Points to Ponder

- Do you know any families who could be included in a study such as the Risman and Myers (1997) study?
- Would these parents' children face the same challenges as the children in the Risman and Myers (1997) study? How did you reach your conclusion?
- What challenges would these children face in the Gum Trees Children's Centre (in the story)?

Points to Discuss

- Do you think that children's experiences of gender inside their family can override their experiences elsewhere? Why do you think this?
- Does each of you think that social attitudes towards gender equity have changed since the Risman and Myers (1997) study? How did you reach your conclusion?
- Which staff member and/parent in the Gum Trees Centre (in the story) is most likely to agree with you? Why do you think this?

Fairness Alert

Early childhood staff can be concerned sometimes about boys who do not behave like 'typical boys'. Like the parents of such boys, some staff want them to be 'just like all the others'. Concerns about these boys can be heightened when the family is from a society or culture that does not tolerate wide variations in how boys can be boys, leading parents and staff to wonder about the consequences if a boy continues to like being different.

The story and the research in this chapter include some examples of an unfair thinking habit called 'essentializing' – seeing an individual as defined by something deep and enduring ('essential') that is associated with their membership of a particular group (e.g. gender, class, sexuality, 'race', ethnicity or culture). Here we examine how gender can be essentialized:

- Essentializing gender by assuming there are essential ways of being a boy or a girl.

Here is an example of essentializing from the story:

> Bonnie: Of course, some ways to be a man are more widespread than others and so they're often described as 'normal' or 'traditional'. But who benefits and who loses from those dominant ways to 'be a man' and are we happy with that?
>
> *Tony:* Look. I want Joe to be strong, brave and confident – just your typical boy. Anyone got a problem with that?

Here are two examples of essentializing from the research literature. The first example is from a Swedish study by Sanberg and Pramling-Samuelsson (2005) about how preschool staff and parents with children in preschools understand co-operation with each others; and the second example is a report of a study of male primary school teachers in England, Sweden and New Zealand (Cushman, 2010).

> This study found that female preschool teachers tend to emphasize care and nurture. Birgerstam (1997) asserts that women are more human relations oriented and men more thing and duty oriented in the profession. For women, it is important to create good relations. Men are more concerned about what they do together with children and how they do it. They want to manage projects in preschool with children; for example, play football.
>
> To sum up the female and male preschool teachers' play code, differences between female and male preschool teachers' play willingness are seen, above all, in participation in play. Men play and are more prepared to engage in physical play. This study found that male preschool teachers contribute with more playfulness, and this is something that both female and male preschool teachers noticed.   (Sanberg and Pramling-Samuelsson, 2005: 304)

According to Matt:

> Boys and girls are different personalities. Girls are eager to please, always want to do jobs for you, where the boys just want to have a laugh with you. So, in that respect, you do respond to the way that they interact with you. Boys are lively and energetic whereas girls are calmer and want to talk at a deeper level (Matt 29-2-08, p.7).
>
> (Cushman, 2010: 1216)

Why essentializing is unfair

- It assumes that boys and girls who lack the 'essential' characteristics of their gender are abnormal and/or strange.
- It denies that boys and girls are individuals with complex ways of 'doing' gender.
- Assuming all men working in childcare have the same skills and interests reinforces inaccurate stereotypes of male early childhood workers.

How you can counter essentializing

- Encourage concerned parents and colleagues to express their concerns about 'non-traditional' boys. This can be a difficult discussion and each person should respect other people's views, however strange they may seem.
- Assume that your assumptions about gender characteristics may be inaccurate.
- Be alert to things that you *do not* know about how specific boys, girls, men and woman think about, 'perform' and experience gender.

Points to Ponder

- Have you experienced men being essentialized?
- What are some common stereotypes of men who work in early childhood education and care settings? How could you challenge these stereotypes? To what extent does *Tony* (in the story) confirm or challenge these stereotypes?

Points to Discuss

- In your experience, what are the advantages and disadvantages of being a non-traditional boy?
- Do you think that early childhood education and care staff have any particular responsibilities around non-traditional boys in their programmes?
- How do you think that *Ruby* (in the story) react if the staff at the Gum Trees Centre tried to support non-traditional boys?

Models of staff–parent relationships around gender education

Here are two models of relationships between families and early childhood staff around the role of early childhood education and care staff in the gender education of young children. Model 1 comes from two research studies in different parts of the world. The first quote is from Karlson's and Simonsson's (2008) study (above) of how preschool staff in Sweden understood their role with parents in implementing gender-sensitive education; the second quote is from a very recent study that asked male primary school teachers in England, Sweden and New Zealand whether their training had prepared them to enter the gendered world of the primary school (Cushman, 2010). Model 2 emerged from a short excerpt from an analysis of preschool gender policies in Scotland and in Sweden (Edström, 2009).

The models are followed by some 'Points to Ponder' and some 'Points to Discuss', which may help you decide what you think about the different approaches to gender education in the story.

> **Model 1: Early childhood education and care staff should initiate provocative discussions about gender equity with parents**

> ... it appears many parents seemed to agree that the gender-sensitive work was important and worth encouraging.
>
> Teacher 2: We even tried to provoke their thoughts, so that they would get the chance to react if they didn't feel comfortable.
>
> Interviewer: What do you mean by 'provoking the parents'?
>
> Teacher 2: This, a little sullen tone, that we heard from Gavle, like 'So, are you going to make my boy gay?'
>
> (Karlson and Simonsson, 2008: 176)

> Jonas said he had learned in his teacher education course that 'thinking about it' was not enough: 'Part of our mission was not to classify sports as female and male sports. In the community, boys play in teams that were once just girls, and girls play in teams that were once boys. I can still meet old-fashioned parents who wish their boy to do boy sports, so I think my work is to erase these traditional lines. I would say my point to parents [is]: my job is to work with the children to erase these traditional ways of seeing sports.' (Jonas 3-3-08, p. 7)
>
> It was clear from this and Jonas's other comments that his declared mission to counteract stereotyping sat comfortably with his personal beliefs. He clearly identified with the view of teachers as 'agents of change' (UNESCO, 2003) and maintained, in line with Francis and Skelton (2001), that teachers need to actively intervene to challenge prevailing images. (Cushman, 2010: 1215)

Model 2: Early childhood education and care staff should be gender equity role models

In both cases, teachers are constructed as role models who should promote certain gender values and provide children with opportunities. The Swedish curriculum places more emphasis on similarities between girls and boys, while the Scottish counterpart tends to emphasize difference more, paying attention to boys and the need for male role models. Scottish gender policies are influenced by the travelling discourse of 'the boys' underachievement crisis', whereas Swedish gender policies in preschool demonstrate little of this. (Edström, 2009: 534)

In the Scottish document, male role models are, in one of the examples from practice, depicted as having a special positive influence on young boys' interest in reading: The centre had a 'Boys and Books Week' when dads and grandpas were invited and encouraged to read from story books before taking their children home. Staff took the time to explain to parents and carers the importance of children seeing men reading and enjoying books. (Scottish Consultative Council on the Curriculum, 1999, p. 22)

(Edström, 2009: 543)

Points to Ponder

- Which model is closer to your own views about gender equity in early childhood education and care programmes?
- Do you think that Bonnie (in the story) was provoking gender equity discussions with the parents?

Points to Discuss

- How would parents and early childhood education and care staff you know react to the idea that staff should 'provoke' gender equity conversations with parents?
- Would you 'provoke' such conversations? Why/Why not?
- Do you think that the Gum Trees staff (in the story) see themselves as gender equity role models, educating parents about gender equity? How did the parents react?

Further reading to deepen your understanding

Freeman, N. (2007) Preschoolers' perceptions of gender appropriate toys and their parents' beliefs about genderized behaviors: miscommunication, mixed messages, or hidden truth. *Early Childhood Education Journal*, 34, 357–66.

Freeman (2007) asked three- and five-year-old boys and girls what they thought were 'girl toys' and 'boy toys' and which of those toys they thought that their parents would let them play with. She then asked parents about their attitudes to gender and toys and compared their responses with the children's. A key finding was that adults give young children mixed messages about gender – what they did around gender equity often contradicted what they told children about it. The article includes a questionnaire (A Child-Rearing Sex-Role Attitude Scale) that could spark discussion between staff and parents.

Lee-Thomas, K., Sumison, J. and Roberts, S. (2005) Teacher understandings of and commitment to gender equity in the early childhood setting. *Australian Journal of Early Childhood*, 30, 21–7.

Lee-Thomas et al. (2005) reported on a study that asked early childhood teachers in Australia how they see their role/s around gender equity. The study found that teachers may be committed to gender equity, but feel pessimistic about achieving it. The authors argue that this may be because of the theoretical framework the teachers used to make sense of gender in children's lives and they suggest ways forward. The article could provoke reflection on how parents and staff understand gender and how their understandings may influence their view of gender equity programs. Can you identify the theory underlying what the adults at the Gum Trees Centre (in the story) think about gender?

References

Cushman, P. (2010) Male primary school teachers: helping or hindering a move to gender equity? *Teaching and Teacher Education*, 26(5): 1211–18.

Edström, C. (2009) Preschool as an arena of gender policies: the examples of Sweden and Scotland. *European Education Research Journal*, 8(4): 534–49.

Freeman, N. (2007) Preschoolers' perceptions of gender appropriate toys and their parents' beliefs about genderized behaviors: miscommunication, mixed messages, or hidden truth. *Early Childhood Education Journal*, 34(5): 357–66.

Karlson, I. and Simonsson, M. (2008) Preschool work teams' view of ways of working with gender – parents' involvement. *Early Childhood Education Journal*, 36(2): 171–7.

Lee-Thomas, K., Sumison, J. and Roberts, S. (2005) Teacher understandings of and commitment to gender equity in the early childhood setting. *Australian Journal of Early Childhood*, 30(1): 21–7.

Risman, B. and Myers, K. (1997) As the twig is bent: children reared in feminist households. *Qualitative Sociology*, 20(2): 229–50.

Sanberg, A. and Pramling-Samuelsson, I. (2005) An interview study of gender differences in preschool teachers' attitudes toward children's play. *Early Childhood Education Journal*, 32(5): 297–305.

15 Lesbian mums – what's the fuss?

The story

To help you quickly grasp who's who, practitioners' names are shown in upright font and parents' names are shown in *italic* font.

An early childhood professional network has organized a day-long conference called 'Children, Families and Diversity', open to staff and parents from early childhood services in its catchment area. One of the concurrent workshops at the conference is called 'Children and Sexuality' and we join it as the workshop leaders – Cheryl and Mandy – are opening the discussion.

Cheryl: Some ten per cent of the population identifies itself as 'non-heterosexual' and so for many young children, the reality is that they will meet and know lesbian and gay people among their parents, early childhood staff, family and friends; and some young children will grow up and identify themselves as gay or lesbian.

Mandy: So in the early childhood world, do we just ignore that? Or do we take it on board, recognise that being gay or lesbian often means being discriminated against and raise that with the children?

Cheryl: Early childhood staff can be cautious about discussing sexuality in their centre, because they want to avoid bad reactions from parents and other people. Do you remember when the ABC's *Playschool** program featured a child with two mums? It was in June 2004. *Playschool* got into a *lot* of trouble in the media, but it was also praised for reflecting the contemporary diversity of family life.

Janet: I remember that program. It referred to the child's 'two mummies', as if homosexual families are as normal as heterosexual ones. So it pushed the line that being homosexual or being heterosexual was a 'lifestyle choice' between equally attractive options. But there isn't a choice. Heterosexuality is *normal* and anything else isn't. I'm sorry, but that's how it is.

Mandy: So do you think that we should stop children from lesbian and gay families from talking about their families? How do you think that children in those families feel when they hear that their family lives are 'abnormal' or 'unnatural'?

Marg: But young children are innocents – they can't understand the complexities of sexual matters. Talk of sexuality has no place in a young child's life – here, in the media or elsewhere. We should protect them from it. That's part of our job.

Cheryl: You say you want to protect 'innocents' from sexuality, but what you really want to do is actively encourage children to see heterosexuality as right and anything else as wrong. That's got to make children fear or hate lesbians and gays.

Janet: No! Parenting is natural, it's biology and the family is a natural unit of a man, his wife and their biological children. So lesbian mothers and gay fathers aren't natural!

Delia: Let me just read you a couple of quotes, here. Lord Acton, the nineteenth-century historian and theologian, said: 'The most certain test by which we judge whether a country is really free is the amount of security enjoyed by minorities.' And the American novelist Rita Mae Brown said, 'The only queer people are those who don't love anybody'.

(Silence)

Lena: I remember that *Playschool* program. I don't know what all the fuss was about. It was just one episode out of – I don't know – thousands, I expect. Yes, it had two mothers, but we didn't see them having to deal with the **heterosexism** and **homophobia** that lesbians and gay people experience every day. As someone just said – it just looked like a personal lifestyle choice. Well it isn't and children need to know that. They need to know that lesbians and gays face stereotyping, harassment, abuse – and violence. They need to know about legal discrimination around property and inheritance. Young children need to know that some people face discrimination like that *and* that they are likely to meet them and possibly be one of them one day.

Jill: Um . . . I hear what you're saying. But, well, we don't have any gay or lesbian parents at my centre, so there isn't really a need to talk about it.

Cheryl: Well, firstly, are you *sure*? Lesbian or gay parents have to be cautious, you know! But secondly, children can benefit from being in an anti-heterosexist environment, irrespective of whether anyone around them identifies as gay or lesbian, just as they can from being an anti-racist and anti-sexist environment. It increases their understanding of diversity and encourages them to be fair to everyone.

(* The ABC [Australian Broadcasting Commission] is the public broadcaster in Australia. *Playschool* is one of its TV programmes for children.)

Resources for thinking and talking about staff–parent relationships

Research Snippets

Here are two snippets from research exploring family diversity and early childhood education and care settings. Research Snippet 1 is from Canadian research in primary and secondary schools that highlights some teachers' difficulties when dealing with families that they consider abnormal (Lasky, 2000). Research Snippet 2 draws on the perspectives and experiences of lesbian families using child care in Sydney, Australia to explore what is considered a normal family (Skattebol and Ferfolja, 2007). Following each Research Snippet are some 'Points to Ponder' and some 'Points to Discuss', which may help you decide how you can address family diversity in ways that support fair and inclusive relationships.

Research Snippet 1: The cultural and emotional politics of teacher-parent interactions (Lasky, 2000)

Lasky (2000) asked 53 teachers from 15 primary and secondary schools of different sizes and levels in Canada how they reacted to parents whom they considered outside 'the norm'.

Some key findings

Teachers felt comfortable with parents who met their expectations and who shared their value systems; and demoralized, angry and discouraged with parents who didn't. Interactions between teachers and parents sometimes left each side feeling confused, misunderstood and powerless. To serve an increasingly diverse population, teachers need appropriate resources and support in their pre-service preparation and continuing professional development and from their school leaders. (Lasky, 2000: 857)

In classrooms and schools, parents play a crucial supplementary role. Parents who do not participate are often seen as inadequate or uncaring, yet most parents who participate are middle-class mothers from two-parent nuclear families (Smith, 1989; Grifith &

Smith, 1986). Why? Perhaps because notions of appropriate family forms and parenting – including relations with schools – vary according to ethnocultural identity (Delpit, 1995; Ogbu, 1993), social class (Vincent & Tomlinson, 1997; Lareau, 1987), and religion (Gibson, 1988). Parents whom teachers regard as 'not normal', as 'uncaring' and as not just 'different' but 'difficult' can evoke incredulity, exasperation and even disgust in teachers.

(Lasky, 2000: 857)

Points to Ponder

- Why do you think that the teachers responded so strongly ('incredulity, exasperation and even disgust') to parents whom they regarded as not normal?
- Do you think that teachers are prepared sufficiently to work in diverse populations?
- How do you think that Mandy (in the story) would respond to these findings?

Points to Discuss

- Can you think of ways in which an early childhood education and care setting that you know sends 'messages' to staff, parents, children and others about what it considers a normal family?
- Do you think it appropriate for early childhood education and care staff to reinforce dominant understandings of 'normal' and 'abnormal' families? How do you think that Cheryl and Janet (in the story) would each answer this question?

Research Snippet 2: Voices from an enclave: lesbian mothers' experiences of child care (Skattebol and Ferfolja, 2007)

Skattebol and Ferfolja (2007) interviewed eight lesbian mothers from Anglo-Celtic, English-speaking backgrounds living in Sydney, Australia whose children attended a childcare centre.

Some key findings

Within the childcare settings used by interviewees, family was generally conceived to be one or two parents who held the responsibility for the routine daily needs of the child. This assumption was apparent to one of the participants, Sam, through the attitudes of childcare staff to the organization of her son's transitions between home and the centre:

> He's always been picked up by lots of different people. I mean this is a really serious thing in relation to how he's figured in [our] community, he doesn't have the one person . . . he's always had a broad range of people coming to get him and take him away. That was quite difficult for [practitioners] to begin with actually, and then they just kind of got used to it . . . Nobody ever actually says, 'That's weird', but what they do is make comments like [shifts to a slightly incredulous tone], 'Is someone getting him today?' or, 'Toby's got a lot of friends or aunties'. . . . I don't think that I'm being paranoid . . . it's just the phrasing of those kind of things [that] indicate that's unusual . . . you know that it's not within their 'normal' range.
>
> Diverse family constellations are not unusual in gay and lesbian communities, in our study, or indeed in the community at large. As Weeks, Heaphy and Donovan (2001, p. 9) point out, family is increasingly "being deployed to denote something broader than the traditional relationships based on lineage, alliance and marriage, referring instead to kin-like networks of relationships, based on friendship, and commitments beyond blood". In gay and lesbian communities, people create different family types in response to feelings of not belonging; a rejection of 'oppressive heterosexual connotations' along with a desire for and a celebration of one's own family/community (Weeks et al., 2001, p. 10).
>
> This shift in family structures and formation is not unique to lesbian- and gay-headed households. Indeed, in her analysis of globalization and its impact on family life, Carrington (2002) suggests that changes in family formations are increasingly common across the broader community. This necessitates significant shifts in thinking for many early childhood practitioners who need to move beyond the idea that there is one family structure they will deal with, or even that family structures are stable through time or space.
>
> (Skattebol and Ferfolja, 2007: 15)

Points to Ponder

- How many different sorts of family can you describe?
- If early childhood education and care staff in a particular setting have only worked with traditional nuclear families, do they need to accept that 'changes in family formations are increasingly common across the broader community'? How do you think that Cheryl (in the story) would answer this question?
- Which of the staff in our story do you think Toby's mother (in Skattebol and Ferfolja, 2007) would feel most comfortable with caring for her child? Why?

Points to Discuss

- Would Sam (in Skattebol and Ferfolja, 2007) and *Marg* (in our story) each feel comfortable that their child was being cared for by a staff member who had 'move(d) beyond the idea that there is one family structure they will deal with'?
- If you were Janet's supervisor, how would you respond to her statement (in the story), 'Heterosexuality is *normal* and anything else isn't. I'm sorry, but that's how it is.' How might Sam (in Skattebol and Ferfolja, 2007) respond to Janet's statement?

 **Fairness Alerts**

As we have seen in the story and in the research literature, discussions about normal and abnormal families often express one or both of two unfair thinking habits – 'privileging' and 'othering'.

'Privileging' means that you see yourself and/or your group as more important than anyone else. Our specific example of privileging in this chapter points to how one form of family life may be privileged over other alternative forms of family life.

- Privileging heterosexual, two parent families over any other form of family.

Here is an example of privileging from the story:

> Janet: Heterosexuality is *normal* and anything else isn't. I'm sorry, but that's how it is.

Here is an example of privileging from the research.

Brody and Stoneman (1981) studied the ways in which fathers and mothers engage in nonverbal contact with their children. They emphasized that they studied 'normal' families and we draw here from their report of research in the field:

> From both a clinical and research perspective, it is interesting that normal families attempt to maintain at least some minimal levels of nonverbal contact.
>
> Previous parent-child relations research has noted that fathers prefer to engage in more physical games and activities with their children while mothers commonly engage their children in verbal and vocal play and play with toys. (Clarke-Stewart, 1978; Yogman, Dixon, Ternick, Als, and Brazelton, Note 1). . . . Mothers and fathers interacted closer with sons. (Brody and Stoneman, 1981: 190–1)

Why privileging is unfair

- It assumes the right to define normal and denies that right to others.
- It reduces other forms of family to 'second class citizens'.
- It equates 'difference' with 'deviance'.

How you can you counter privileging

- Assume that each group has an equal right to its ideas, values and way of life.
- Offer children stories, games and videos of people in diverse relationships, including different sorts of families.
- Include pictures of notable lesbians and gay men among the images around the service or centre and in its publicity and publications.
- Make a particular point of inviting parents or staff who identify as gay or lesbian to discuss your programme.

Points to Ponder

- To which gender, class, ethnic or cultural groups did/does your family belong? Has this affected your life in any way?
- Have you experienced heterosexual, two-parent families being 'privileged'? Did other families respond in any way? How did you respond? Would your response be the same if it happened again?

Points to Discuss

- Do you think that the normal family (however defined) should be privileged over other family types?
- If every family type is seen as equally valid and none is defined as abnormal, are there any implications for notions of normal child development? How do you think that *Lena* (in the story) would answer this question?

Othering means that you see yourself and/or your group as the norm, from which everyone else deviates. In what follows we examine instances of othering in relation to what is considered a family:

- Othering people who live in abnormal families.

Here is an example of othering from the story:

> Janet: No! Parenting is natural, it's biology and the family is a natural unit of a man, his wife and their biological children. So lesbian mothers and gay fathers are unnatural!

Skattebol and Ferfolja (2007) studied lesbian parents' experiences when their children attended early childhood education and care settings in Sydney (Australia). In our example of othering one of the participants in that study describes how she felt when staff wanted to have a photographic display of children's families at her children's centre:

> (The staff) want photos of how people constitute their families, which is actually a really good thing. . . . (Y)ou can see that they're trying . . . 'Here we've got different families', but actually for me, all that does is reinscribe the fact that (Declan's) not in that model. . . .

If I had a photo of his family, there would be maybe five people, six people . . . there's a part of me that just doesn't want a picture with him and Maeve and I, because that's not his family . . .

(Skattebol and Ferfolja, 2007: 16)

Why othering is unfair

- It promotes one family type as the norm, yet offers no evidence that this makes it superior to other family types.

How you can you counter othering

- Welcome differences in families as normal and desirable – do not assume that a particular family type is the norm.
- Accept that a child may regard a lesbian or gay family as normal and desirable.
- Accept that lesbian and gay families – like all families – will differ in structure, lifestyle and values.
- Consider changing your view of the normal family if it hurts or offends people who do not share it.
- Challenge statements and actions that 'other' families with lesbian and gay parents.
- Create environments where all children feel that their families are respected and where all children can learn to respect diversity.
- Do not assume that someone (child or adult) is or will be of a particular sexuality.
- Discuss diversity, difference and discrimination with children and adults where and when appropriate.
- When possible, use inclusive language (e.g. 'parent' or 'carer', rather than 'mother' or 'father'; 'dominant' or 'widespread', rather than 'normal').

Points to Ponder

- Was/is your family normal or abnormal? Has this affected your life in any way?
- Have you experienced othering (of yourself or of someone else)?
- Does othering do anything more than just point out, 'They're different'?

Points to Discuss

- Have you othered someone else? Who were they and why did you other them?
- Does othering do anything more than just privilege one family type over others? How do you think that *Lena* (in the story) would answer this question?

Models of staff–parent relationships around family diversity

In the field of early childhood education and care, much of the discussion around lesbian and gay families revolves around condemnation of the abnormal versus celebration of diversity. Below are two models of family types that capture this dichotomy. Model 1 underpins the critique of 'normality' by UK academic Victoria Clarke and consists of two quotes: one from an article on how lesbian parents appeared in the psychological literature between 1886 and 2006 (Clarke, 2008); the other from an article which explored how the media and six focus groups of university students saw lesbian and gay parents (Clarke, 2001). Model 2 celebrates family diversity and so it is fitting that it consists of quotes from quite different sources: the first is from a textbook for early childhood professionals published in the USA; the second quote is from an Australian research study of the experiences of lesbian mothers whose children attend early childhood education and care settings (Skattebol, 2007) and it highlights the complex negotiations undertaken by those mothers and their children as they interact with **heteronormative** thinking and **homophobia**.

The models are followed by some 'Points to Ponder' and some 'Points to discuss', which may help you decide what you think about the different attitudes to sexuality, diversity, normality and families expressed by the characters in the story.

Model 1: Lesbian and gay families are not normal

Harne et al. (1997: 30, cited in Clarke, 2008) identified two central assumptions of the psychological literature: that 'it is preferable for children to grow up to be heterosexual rather than lesbian or gay' and that 'it is better for children to conform to . . . gender stereotypes'.   (Clarke, 2008: 125)

> Moreover, lesbian motherhood continues to be regarded as a departure from the norm even in affirmative contexts, mothers are assumed to be heterosexual unless otherwise stated.
>
> (Clarke, 2008: 124)

Thematic analysis of recent media representations of lesbian and gay parenting and six focus groups with university students highlighted the repeated use of a number of arguments to oppose lesbian and gay parenting. I critically discuss the six most prevalent in this article. These are: (1) "The Bible tells me that lesbian and gay parenting is a sin"; (2) "Lesbian and gay parenting is unnatural"; (3) "Lesbian and gay parents are selfish because they ignore 'the best interests of the child' "; (4) "Children in lesbian and gay families lack appropriate role models"; (5) "Children in lesbian and gay families grow up lesbian and gay"; and (6) "Children in lesbian and gay families get bullied."

(Clarke, 2001: 555)

Model 2: Family diversity is normal

Margaret Smith's third-grade classroom has a mix of family groups. Some of her parents had children as young teens and others waited until much later in life. One of Margaret's families is homeless, several qualify for food stamps and a few are upper middle class. Several single-parent families, remarriages and a gay couple add further diversity to her family configurations. Ethnic and religious differences create an even more varied mix of values, attitudes, and traditions among her families.　　　　(Henniger, 2009: 182)

We had been in one centre that was very proactive about gay and lesbians but moved our child to another centre for various reasons. The new centre was strong on cultural diversity but was located in a much more conservative community and we were unsure how the gay and lesbian thing would go with the other kids and families. I have to say it was great. The new centre involved families all the time on a whole lot of levels, so there was heaps of opportunities for us to actually sit down and talk with families informally. It's hard to be scared of lesbians when you are all talking about getting kids to eat their dinner, or speed humps in the road. . . . Jim was invited for a play date very quickly and the note was addressed to 'Jim's Mums' – clearly someone had made it clear to the family we were lesbians and the family had been sensitive enough to realise that we might wonder whether (they knew that) Jim had two mums . . .

(Skattebol, 2007: 59)

Points to Ponder

- Is difference in families necessarily abnormal? Do you think that people's view of normal/abnormal families depend on their experiences of diversity in family life?
- Do you think that Janet (in the story) would accept that 'It's hard to be scared of lesbians when you are all talking about getting kids to eat their dinner, or speed humps in the road.' (Skattebol, 2007: 59)?

Points to Discuss

- In general terms, what's wrong with being abnormal?
- If someone disagrees fundamentally with you, are they abnormal . . . or are you?

Further reading to deepen your thinking and talking

Giovacco-Johnson, T. (2009) Portraits of partnership: the hopes and dreams project. *Early Childhood Education Journal*, 37(2): 127–35.

Giovacco-Johnson (2009) describes *The Hopes and Dreams Project*, which used narrative inquiry to help families in a diverse school community share their lives, their priorities for their children and their desires to be involved in the school community. It offers ways to increase communication between diverse families within a specific educational community. How might the families in Skattebol's (2007) study felt in this project?

LGBT Early Childhood Initiative (n.d.) Quality Child Care for Children of Lesbian, Gay, Bisexual, Transgender Parents: A Checklist for Parents and Caregivers. San Francisco, Lesbian Gay Bisexual and Transgender Early Childhood Initiative.

LGBT Early Childhood Initiative (n.d.) offers a good checklist of inclusive approaches to the education and care of young children whose parents are lesbian, gay, bisexual or transgendered. What elements of the checklist do you think are relevant in your circumstances? Which of the characters in the story would welcome the checklist?

References

Brody, G. and Stoneman, Z. (1981) Parental nonverbal behavior within the family context. *Family Relations*, 30(2): 187–90.

Clarke, V. (2001) What about the children? Arguments against lesbian and gay parenting. *Women's Studies International Forum*, 24(5): 555–70.

Clarke, V. (2008) From outsiders to motherhood to reinventing the family: constructions of lesbian parenting in the psychological literature – 1886–2006. *Women's Studies International Forum*, 31(2): 118–28.

Giovacco-Johnson, T. (2009) Portraits of partnership: the hopes and dreams project. *Early Childhood Education Journal*, 37(2): 127–35.

Henniger, M. (2009) *Teaching young children: An introduction* (4th edn). Upper Saddle River, NJ and Columbus, OH: Merrill, an imprint of Pearson.

Lasky, S. (2000) The cultural and emotional politics of teacher-parent interactions. *Teaching and Teacher Education*, 16(8): 843–60.

LGBT Early Childhood Initiative (n.d.) *Quality Child Care for Children of Lesbian, Gay, Bisexual, Transgender Parents: A Checklist for Parents and Caregivers*. Report for Lesbian Gay Bisexual and Transgender Early Childhood Initiative, San Francisco.

Skattebol, J. (2007) Through their mother's eyes: the impact of heteronormative paradigms in child care on lesbian- and gay-headed families. *International Journal of Equity and Innovation in Early Childhood*, 5(2): 47–63.

Skattebol, J. and Ferfolja, T. (2007) Voices from an enclave: lesbian mothers' experiences of child care. *Australian Journal of Early Childhood*, 32(1): 10–18.

16 Are we genuine partners and how do we know?

To help you quickly grasp who's who, practitioners' names are shown in upright font and parents' names are shown in *italic* font.

Lydia is a qualified early childhood teacher who has worked at the Brookview Children's Centre for several years. She is keen to involve parents in the Centre's curriculum and has initiated various forms of communication with parents in order to do so. However, she feels that parents are still not involved sufficiently and today, as on several previous occasions, she's discussing this problem with her colleagues.

Lydia: I don't think that we're involving the parents in our program as much as we ought to.

Norma: Come on, Lydia. We've got the newsletter, the notice board and the parent-teacher nights; and we've also got the 'Room Journals' and the 'Communication Books'. What more can we do?!

Lydia: But parents rarely write anything in the 'Room Journals' . . .

Norma: . . . but they talk more about them when the books include photos of their children.

Lydia: . . . and as for the 'Communication Books', well, some parents use them to say how their child should spend her/his time each day. Now, we want to respect these parents' wishes, OK, but if we do, then we take away the children's chance to have a say in how their day looks.

Joan: And some parents write in the 'Communication Books' about any problems they're having with their children, so the whole the Centre ends up knowing about it, rather than just the relevant staff.

Lydia: So it's not working properly.

Roz: Everyone says that they include parents' views in their program, but in practice they only include the voices that more or less agree with them. And look, I don't like to admit it, but I certainly spend more time with some parents than with others – just because I find them easier to get on with than some others.

Norma: And we all know who the others are, don't we?! (Laughter)

Lydia: There's certainly some children – and adults – that I naturally gravitate towards, but others I have difficulty connecting with. So my relationships with children can depend on how I feel about their parents, but how I feel about the child can affect how I feel about their parents.

Joan: Don't be so hard on yourself, Lydia – we can't get on with everyone.

Lydia still worried that the ideal of parents and staff being partners was not working in practice, so she decided to distribute a brief (two questions!) questionnaire to parents. (She felt that, in hindsight, she should have asked the children for their views, too.) She presented the results of the questionnaire to a staff meeting.

Lydia: Question 1 was: 'How do you see parent involvement at the centre?' Everyone felt that parent-staff relationships were generally positive and they felt able to say how they felt about their children's time at the centre. They liked the daily chat with the teacher as they arrived and left, as well as the more in-depth conversations at social events and parent/teacher nights. Many parents said that the children's individual books were a good way to learn about their child's day, their development, their interests, etc.; and that this information was complemented by the 'Room Journals' and by the displays of children's pictures and work. They also said that if teachers and parents are open with each other, they can share their ideas about how to care for children.

Roz: Hmmm. So everything's fine, then Lydia. Nothing to worry about.

Norma: You know, while I was talking to the parents as I gave them their questionnaire and when they returned them, I started to get a much better idea of their daily stresses and struggles. I suppose I hadn't really thought about it before. So now I try to sort of step back a bit and reserve judgement on what parents say and do. And I'm less flippant with them – you know, when you tell them 'Everything's fine' as they leave their child in a screaming heap at the beginning of the day! Now I often just e-mail them or give them a call to let them know that their child has settled.

Lydia: Question 2 was: 'How can staff include parents' and children's voices in our curriculum in meaningful and respectful ways?' Parents said that children's voices can be heard through their art work and through the children's individual daily journals; and that parents' voices van be included via the social events and meetings. They also said that staff could e-mail draft curriculum ideas to parents for comment.

Joan: To do that sort of work – including parents' and children's views – you need the current research about curriculum, for a start. Also, I don't think that it's something that you can do by yourself, Lydia. I think that you need to link with other people who are doing similar work with families.

Resources for thinking and talking about staff–parent relationships

Research Snippets

Here are two snippets from the research concerning teachers' and parents' attitudes to parent involvement programmes. Research Snippet 1 is from a study of Israeli teachers' attitudes – positive and negative – to parent involvement and why they encourage it (Addi-Raccah and Ainhoren, 2009). Research Snippet 2 is from a study of how parents in the USA felt about being surveyed about their views and experiences in an early childhood programme (Bailey and Blasso, 1990). The study was conducted in 1990, but it is included because 10 years later, parents are still being asked to participate in such surveys.

Following each Research Snippet are some 'Points to Ponder' and some 'Points to Discuss' that may help you decide how you might answer Lydia's question in the story, ' How can staff include parents' and children's voices in our curriculum in meaningful and respectful ways?'

Research Snippet 1: School governance and teachers' attitudes to parents' involvement in schools (Addi-Raccah and Ainhoren, 2009)

This study of Israeli teachers' attitudes towards parent involvement had 318 participants – head teachers, chairpersons of parents' committees, and teachers – from 11 primary schools. Participants completed a questionnaire that explored their personal and occupational characteristics, how empowered they felt in their work, the nature of parental influence on their work and the frequency and nature of their contacts with the parents of the children in their schools. Head teachers and the chairs of parent committees were also interviewed.

Some key findings

- Early career teachers struggled most to build positive relationships with parents, often because they felt overwhelmed by the complexity of their work and less certain about their professional skills than more experienced teachers.
- The most positive parent involvement happened when teachers and parents had a strong voice in what happened within the schools:

From this stance, both parents and teachers might collaborate and establish mutual interests. This supports the view of the school partnership mode of governance as a promising step toward a community-oriented approach that may foster school improvement (Warren, 2005). In this regard, the research findings are challenging and quite optimistic due to the ongoing recommendation for parent–school partnerships, which characterize successful and communitarian school settings (Leithwood and Riehl, 2003). This, however, does not seem to occur as a result of top-down reform, but rather through the collaboration and mutual influences between parents, teachers, and school leaders that are cultivated at the school site (Marks and Nance, 2007). In this regard empowering parents and teachers is not a zero sum game. Both sides appear to benefit from having influence at school.

(Addi-Raccah and Ainhoren, 2009: 811)

Points to Ponder

- To what extent do you think that a teacher's experience might influence their approach to parent involvement?
- In your own experience, what sorts of teachers involve parents successfully in their programmes?

Points to Discuss with another adult

- Do you think that the findings by Addi-Raccah and Ainhoren (2009) reflect the discussion between Roz and Norma in the story about how some staff gravitate to some parents?
- In your experience, is parent involvement more successful when it is initiated by staff or by parents?

Research Snippet 2: Parents' perspectives on a written survey of family needs (Bailey and Blasso, 1990)

Bailey and Blasso (1990) used a postal survey to explore parents' attitudes to using The Family Needs Survey. In other words, it was a survey about parents' attitudes to being surveyed! The participants were 229 parents (primarily mothers) or other carers of young children with disabilities in 10 states in the USA.

Some key findings

Nearly 60 per cent of the mothers surveyed preferred talking to early childhood education and care staff, rather than completing surveys. More specifically: 68 per cent of minority group mothers preferred talking to staff, while 53 per cent of the white mothers preferred talking to staff. As one mother explained:

> I truly believe that a sensitive professional or experienced parent with good communication skills, who had their own list of topics so as not to leave out any, could just sit down with the family . . . and have a discussion about needs and services. Why does that seem so impossible? I am so tired of checklists and circling the number corresponding to statements that are not mine, and then some other professional making an interpretation or judgment based on that.
> (Bailey and Blasso, 1990: 201)

Some parents expressed frustration at not being told what happened to the information that they had provided in the survey. As one mother said:

> After you have been in different programs and dealing with so many 'professionals', you get so sick and tired of saying the same thing over and over. I'm not a hateful person, but I hate to do questionnaires and evaluations where no one does anything about it.
> (Bailey and Blasso, 1990: 202)

Points to Ponder

- Do you find the researchers' findings surprising? Why? (Why not?)
- Why do you think that the white and minority group parents differed in their preference for verbal communication with staff?
- Do you think that these findings link with Norma's statement (in the story) that, 'You know, while I was talking to the parents as I gave them their questionnaire and when they returned them, I started to get a much better idea of their daily stresses and struggles'?

Points to Discuss

- Do you prefer verbal or written communication? In your experience of early childhood education and care settings, what are the pros and cons of each method (a) for staff and (b) for parents?
- Do you think that Lydia's survey (in the story) was the best way for her to find out what involvement parents want in the programme? Why? Why not?

Fairness Alert

The story and the Research Snippets include some examples of an unfair thinking habit called 'silencing' – making it difficult for an individual or a group to be seen and/or heard. The emphasis in this chapter is on the dynamics of silencing parents' voices in the early childhood curriculum:

- Silencing parents' voices in curriculum decision-making.

Here is an example of silencing from the story:

Roz: Everyone says that they include parents' views in their program, but in practice they only include the voices that more or less agree with them. And look, I don't like to admit it, but I certainly spend more time with some parents than with others – just because I find them easier to get on with than some others.

Norma: And we all know who the others are, don't we?! (Laughter)

Lydia: There's certainly some children – and adults – that I naturally gravitate towards, but others I have difficulty connecting with. So my relationships with children can depend on how I feel about their parents, but how I feel about the child can affect how I feel about their parents.

Joan: Don't be so hard on yourself, Lydia – we can't get on with everyone.

Here is an example of silencing from the research about parents' involvement. It is an extract from a letter to parents in Germany whose children are using a particular mathematics textbook (*Der Zahlenbuch*). Teachers can photocopy the letter from the book to introduce their mathematics curriculum to parents.

> You support your child's development of independent learning best if you let her or him do the homework on her or his own, interfering as little as possible. Apart from that, trust your child's teacher. You need have no worries as far as this is concerned. Our school enjoys its good reputation precisely because of the high level of competence of its teachers. (Gellert, 2005: 320)

Why silencing is unfair

- Practices as well as words can silence views and perspectives when they do not invite alternative ideas or views to be expressed.
- Communication that is one-way (e.g. 'telling' or 'informing') implies that other people's views are not wanted and/or are irrelevant.
- It assumes/implies that there is a hierarchy of knowledge, with professional knowledge at the top.
- It relies on and reinforces professionals defining the hierarchy of knowledge, preventing other types of knowledge from reaching the top.
- It implies that professionals produce knowledge and that non-professionals' role is merely to be grateful.

How you can counter silencing

- Assume that parents from all ethnic, cultural and language groups have valuable ideas and views about their children's education that could be helpful to staff.

- Actively encourage individuals and groups to express their ideas and views about young children's education and care and welcome them as valid.
- Actively create circumstances where holders of 'non-mainstream' views about young children feel comfortable expressing them and where their ideas are treated with respect. Do not assume that you have succeeded in doing so – always ask.
- Be prepared to rethink your ideas about young children's education and care if they fail to reflect the experiences of families with whom you work.
- Try to use 'different from', rather than 'better than' when comparing and contrasting different sources and types of knowledge about young children.
- If you encounter ideas and practices that you find unacceptable, explain your position, rather than just assert it as a professional . . . and be prepared to rethink your position if circumstances change.

Points to Ponder

- Who did Norma and Joan (in the story) 'silence' and how did each of them do it?
- If you read that your child's school 'enjoys its good reputation precisely because of the high level of competence of its teachers', would you feel comfortable asking the teachers to change how they behaved with your child?

Points to Discuss

- When is one-way communication (telling or informing) by a teacher appropriate? When is it inappropriate?
- Do you tend to pay more attention in early childhood education and care settings to some sorts of people than to others? What sorts of people are they in each case? (Be honest!)

Models of (genuine) staff–parent partnerships

Here are two models of staff-parent partnerships, each based on current debates in the early childhood literature about the nature of staff-parent partnerships. The models are followed by some 'Points to Ponder' and some 'Points to Discuss', which may help you decide what you think 'works properly' to involve parents in a child's programme.

Model 1 equates partnership with parent empowerment and it underpins excerpts from two articles. The first article (Ng, 2007) identifies five phases of parent empowerment in schools in Hong Kong and suggests that teachers in Hong Kong have resisted such parent empowerment. The second article (Morrow and Malin, 2004) describes a study of parent participation in the UK's Sure Start programme. Model 2 equates partnership with informal communication – 'yacking' – and is expressed in a small qualitative study of parent support in early childhood education centres in New Zealand (Duncan et al., 2006). Each model is followed by some 'Points to Ponder' and some 'Points to Discuss', which may help you decide what you think makes for genuine partnerships between parents and staff in early childhood education and care settings.

Model 1: In genuine partnerships, parents are empowered decision-makers

---

> (In Hong Kong, there have been) five phases of development of parent empowerment which include (1) the period of absolute quiescence and acquiescence; (2) the period of wakefulness of parents' rights and responsibilities, (3) the period of enhancing communication; (4) the period of accountability; and (5) the period of parents as partners. (Ng, 2007: 487)

> Since the passing of the Education Bill, parents are empowered to be involved at different levels of school operation . . . Not only are they encouraged to get involved in their children's education outside school as supervisors at home but they are also invited to be school managers and advisers inside school. According to Ng (2006) and Edward (1995), when parents are empowered to be involved in the decision making process, they can be treated as school partners in which mutual respect and recognition are of paramount significance. (Ng, 2007: 496)

> . . . partnership implies equality and a division of power that draws parents into decision-making and policy issues, going beyond helping and information sharing. (Morrow and Malin, 2004: 164)

Model 2: In genuine partnerships, parents can have a 'good yack'

To "yack" has been defined as "to talk continuously, especially informally" (Cambridge Dictionary, 2004). This informal and regular chatting and conversations (gossips and yacks) between those working in and attending the EC centres has been identified, in this study, as an important type of regular contact between teachers and families, and was identified by families as a direct support for parents and their children.   (Duncan et al., 2006: 2)

From a parent:

So it is not just like frivolous conversation – she is actually really taking in what is happening in my life. . . . It tells me that we matter to the centre and they understand people's feelings. They don't see parents walking in the door as just business . . .

(Duncan et al., 2006: 8)

Points to Ponder

- Which model of (genuine) partnerships is closer to yours?
- Are these models mutually exclusive or do you think that empowered parents in genuine partnerships can still 'yack' with staff?
- Which of the staff at Brookview children's centre (in the story) do you think would be most in favour of 'yacking' with parents to build stronger partnerships with them? How did you reach your conclusion?

Points to Discuss with another adult

- What do you think marks out a *genuine* partnership between parents and staff in early childhood education and care settings? Are such partnerships easy to create?
- What would you advise the Brookview Children's Centre staff (in the story) to do in order to create genuine partnerships with parents in their centre?

Further reading to deepen your understanding

Roeflofs, E., Visser, J. and Terwel, J. (2002) Preferences for various learning environments: teachers' and parents' perceptions. *Learning Environments Research*, 6(1): 77–110.

Roeflofs et al. (2002) describe a study in the Netherlands that asked students, teachers and parents whether they preferred direct instruction, discovery learning or authentic pedagogy. Participants came from primary, secondary and secondary-vocational schools, but staff and parents in early childhood education and care settings who wish to build genuine partnerships could use the researchers' two detailed research instruments to build shared understandings of teaching and learning. You may like to reflect on how helpful (or not) these instruments might be to the staff at Brookview Children's Centre (in the story). Which of the Brookview staff do you think would be most likely to use these instruments?

Arti, J., Eberly, J. and Konzal, J. (2005) Dialogue across cultures: teachers' perceptions about communication with diverse families. *Multicultural Education*, 13(2): 11–15.

Arti et al. (2005) asked preschool to grade 3 teachers in the USA how they build partnerships with parents in ethnically diverse communities. The teachers said that they valued meetings with parents, but in fact they relied more on giving parents printed information, rather than asking their views or learning from them. What aspects of the findings by Arti et al. (2005) do you think would help the staff (in the story) at the Brookview children's centre to build partnerships with parents? You may also like to reflect on the links between the findings by Arti et al. (2005) and the other research projects you have read about in this chapter.

References

Addi-Raccah, A. and Ainhoren, R. (2009) School governance and teachers' attitudes to parents' involvement in schools. *Teaching and Teacher Education*, 25(2): 805–13.

Arti, J., Eberly, J. and Konzal, J. (2005) Dialogue across cultures: teachers' perceptions about communication with diverse families. *Multicultural Education*, 13(2): 11–15.

Bailey, D. and Blasso, R. (1990) Parents' perspectives on a written survey of family needs. *Journal of Early Intervention*, 14(3): 196–203.

Duncan, J., Bowden, C. and Smith, A. (2006) A gossip or a good yack? Reconceptualizing parent support in New Zealand early childhood centre based programme. *International Journal of Early Years Education*, 14(1): 1–13.

Gellert, U. (2005) Parents: support or obstacle for curriculum innovation? *Journal of Curriculum Studies*, 37(3): 313–28.

Morrow, G. and Malin, N. (2004) Parents and professionals working together: turning the rhetoric into reality. *Early Years*, 24(2): 163–77.

Ng, S.-W. (2007) The chronological development of parent empowerment in children's education in Hong Kong. *Asia Pacific Education Review*, 8(3): 487–99.

Roeflofs, E., Visser, J. and Terwel, J. (2002) Preferences for various learning environments: teachers' and parents' perceptions. *Learning Environments Research*, 6(1): 77–110.

17 That's jargon to me!

To help you quickly grasp who's who, practitioners' names are shown in upright font and parents' names are shown in *italic* font.

Amber was concerned that she limited parents' involvement in her centre to what she believed is appropriate. On reflection, she realized that she had given no thought to her communication with parents in her centre, because she regarded them as 'well educated' – like her. However, when a parent told her that her early childhood jargon intimidated parents sometimes, Amber wondered whether she had assumed too much in her relationships with parents. She discussed her concerns with her friend Rachel, an early childhood researcher at the nearby university.

Amber: We had a staff meeting last week about involving parents more and a couple of people said that it was difficult because parents tend to talk just about their specific child, whereas we use our early childhood background to talk about children in general. They said that if parents learnt more about child development, they'd be more able to participate in what we're doing.

Rachel: Did you agree?

Amber: I know what they meant . . . but maybe it's our early childhood jargon that's the problem – you know, 'cognitive development', 'stages', 'outcomes'. I want to understand what families want for the children, but I'm afraid that if I just ask them, they'll say what they think I want them to . . . or they won't even say anything. What can I do?

Rachel: When you talk to parents about their children, try to keep your question as 'open' as possible to different answers. So don't ask a 'technical' question about child development. Ask something broader, something that they might ask themselves.

Amber: Hmmm! Stop thinking as an early childhood person after eleven years in the job! (Pensive)

Rachel: How about asking them how they'd like other people to see their child?

Amber: Even better! Ask them how they'd like to see their child as a grown-up. Something like this: 'When your child reaches the age of 21 and you give a speech at their 21st birthday party, how would you like to describe them?' Is that an 'open' question?

Rachel: Absolutely! It leaves the parents free to decide how *they* would like to talk about their children. Good question, Amber!

A month later, Amber met Rachel again and told her what had been happening.

Amber: It was really good! Parents said that it was nice to think about what they wanted for their child beyond just the next couple of years. Many parents said that what was important to them was their children's social and emotional development. They wanted their child to be 'popular', 'respectful' and 'happy', to have good relationships with a range of people and to have good and supportive friends and family.

Rachel: Simply – they wanted their children to love and be loved.

Amber: That's right. Reading their responses to my question made me really think about and value parents. On the whole, we all want the same thing. . . . It seems to me that over the eleven years that I have been in early childhood, our focus has shifted from nurturing and caring to more academic-type learning. We're too concerned about academic development at the expense of other types of development. We're obsessed with teaching children, rather than just being with them and nurturing them and helping their social and emotional sides. For us, it's always, 'We must complete out tasks! We must achieve results!'

Rachel: Did many parents respond to your question?

Amber: That was the other thing – lots of the parents who responded had kept themselves pretty much to themselves before.

Rachel: Perhaps they felt more comfortable having this type of conversation?

Amber: Who knows? But if that *is* the case, then what does that say about my communication with them in the past, you know? When I talk with them in what is normal language for me, they don't respond;

but when I ask them an open-ended question, out it all comes. Parents who've never said much before about their children suddenly had lots to say. So how must they have felt before?

Rachel: So what do you think the implications are for how you work now?

Amber: Well, I guess the first thing is that I've got to remember that the early childhood way to understand children isn't the only way and it isn't necessarily the right way. And I think that links with my feeling that we're focusing too much on 'academic' learning and not enough on the social and emotional sides. . . . And even if early childhood *is* the right way to understand children, what I've seen is that it's preventing some parents from talking about their children when they come here. And that's not good.

Resources for thinking and talking about staff–parent relationships

Research Snippets

Here are two snippets from the extensive research about the importance of shared understandings between parents and staff about what is important for children. Research Snippet 1 comes from a small-scale qualitative study in Australia of parents' perspectives on their involvement in their children's education and care (Elliott, 2003). Research Snippet 2 is taken from a study in the USA of the factors that contribute to positive relationships between staff and parents in early childhood education and care settings (Blue-Banning et al., 2004).

Following each Research Snippet are some 'Points to Ponder' and some 'Points to Discuss', which may help you decide what you think about the effect of professional language on staff–parent relationships.

Research Snippet 1: Sharing care and education: parents' perspectives (Elliott, 2003)

Elliott (2003) conducted five focus group interviews with 36 parents from 13 early childhood centres in socially and economically diverse contexts in Sydney, asking them about their involvement in their children's early childhood settings.

Some key findings

- Many parents felt unable to influence their child's education and care because of the lack of effective communication by early childhood staff. For example:

  An area of vexation for parents was the written weekly program. Animated discussions took place in all focus groups, with the following comment a distillation of the discourse: 'I look at the program but, you know, I don't get the end result. It's like the book is open but you can't turn the page. You know it's written there but what went before, what happened to these activities, did my child participate? How did he go? What was the point of the activity? It's all very secretive. There is a code on the program – "C3" – but I don't know what that means . . . Is it my child? What is it there for? Who knows what it means?' (F4:R).

  It appears that staff in services used by these parents provide written information about the programs provided for children. Yet failure to provide explanations or follow-up information meant parents were unable to interpret what the staff were trying to share with them. (Elliott, 2003: 18)

Points to Ponder

- What are the implications of this study for (a) staff and (b) parents?
- If you are a student or staff member, what aspects of your work do you think you might need to interpret to parents?
- If you are a parent, have you encountered language in early childhood programmes that you did not 'get'? What did you do?

Points to Discuss

- Do parents and staff sometimes lack a common language in which to talk about young children and early childhood programs?
- Did Amber (in the story) discover a common language in which to talk with parents, or did she discover that her professional language was ineffective?

Snippet 2: Dimensions of family and professional partnerships: constructive guidelines for collaboration (Blue-Banning et al., 2004)

Blue-Banning et al. (2004) explored how to create positive partnerships between parents and professionals in early childhood education and care in the USA. They conducted 33 focus groups with adult family members of children with and without disabilities and service providers and administrators; and 32 individual interviews with non-English-speaking parents and their service providers. The researchers then themed participants' responses and identified similarities and differences between them.

Some key findings

The researchers identified six main features of positive staff–parent partnerships: communication, commitment, equality, skills, trust and respect. More specifically the study participants emphasized that partnership requires equality or reciprocity between families and service providers. An equal partnership includes a sense of harmony or ease in the relationship. Family members often expressed this concept by describing positive relationships with professionals whom they considered 'down to earth', as in this mother's description:

> She's very educated . . . but you would never know it. . . . . You know, some people when they have those degrees, they are here up in the air and, you know, 'You be little, you beneath me.' But she's not that type of person. She's a down-to-earth person.

Beyond simply promoting an easy or harmonious relationship, the study participants believed that establishing equality required active effort from professionals to empower families. They described the importance of having professionals acknowledge the validity of parents' points of view, as opposed to discounting or in private, avoiding implications of blame, and remembering to include positive comments about a child as well as the challenges. Communication, according to these participants, should also be clear and free of jargon.   (Blue-Banning et al., 2004: 176–7)

Many professionals said they needed to avoid jargon in their communication. They also emphasized the need to check tactfully to make sure that all parents, especially possible non-readers, understood the reports, description of rights, and other documents they were receiving:

> You're going over your paperwork and you notice, you're looking at them, they're not reading. And then you [think] . . . 'Oh, this man can't read or not read very well' . . . And then you can tell the therapist on the file without, you know, causing any embarrassment and they can get ways to show them the information.   (Blue-Banning et al., 2004: 175)

Points to Ponder

- Is it inevitable that conversations between staff and parents about their children will feature at least some professional or technical terms? How do you think that Amber (in the story) might respond to your answer?
- Do you think that some parents might say that they understand professional or technical terms when they do not? How could staff discover whether this was happening?

Points to Discuss

- Is the use of professional or technical terms a mark of professional expertise? If it is, should parents be expected to learn what the terms mean? If it is not, why do professionals use such terms?
- In your experience, do some parents respond more easily and comfortably than others to staff who use professional or technical terms?

Fairness Alerts

The story and the research literature around language issues between staff and parents each feature examples of two unfair thinking habits – 'privileging' and 'othering'. 'Privileging' means that you see yourself and/or your group as more important than anyone else. In this specific instance we focus on privileging language:

- Privileging professional language as more accurate and valuable than everyday language.

Here is an example of privileging from the story:

> Amber: We had a staff meeting last week about involving parents more and a couple of people said that it was difficult because parents tend to talk just about their specific child, whereas we use our early childhood background to talk about children in general.

Here is an example of privileging from the research. It comes from a study of two schools in the USA that were introducing the Reggio Emilia philosophy of teaching and learning; and how eight teachers in these schools negotiated with parents who complained that the innovation reduced the curriculum's 'academic' content (Sisson, 2009). One teacher, Alison, said:

> It's like talking to someone who only has one word for what they need to say and what they need to say is very complex and it's about their child, but all that they can come up with is the word, 'academic'.

The researcher wrote:

> Alison suggested that parents often do not understand the complexities of child development and learning. (Sisson, 2009: 360)

Why privileging is unfair

- It assumes the right to say that conversations will feature professional, technical terms and denies that right to others.
- It reduces anyone who does not use professional, technical terms to 'second-class citizens' whose views are less valid or meaningful.
- It equates 'inexperienced' with 'inadequate'.

How you can counter privileging

- Assume that each group has an equal right to its ideas, values and way of life and to the means by which it expresses them.
- Express yourself in ways that do not rely on professional, technical terms and ask people if they understand you.
- Ask the people with whom you talk to identify jargon in your conversations. Do not just assume that you know – one person's everyday speech can be another person's impenetrable jargon.

Points to Ponder

- To which gender, class, ethnic or cultural groups did/do you belong? Has this affected the language you use to talk about children?
- Have you experienced a particular form of language (e.g. medical, engineering) being privileged over others? How did people who used other forms of language respond? How did you respond? Would your response be the same in another instance of privileging?

Points to Discuss

- Do you think that professional, technical language has a place in early childhood and care settings? How do you think that Amber (in the story) would answer this question?
- Is jargon ever justified? If it is, then shouldn't people learn what it means? If it is not, then why do people persist in using it?

'Othering' means that you see yourself and/or your group as the norm, from which everyone else deviates. In this specific example we focus on othering language:

- Othering people who don't understand/use the professional, technical language of early childhood education and care.

Here is an example from of othering from the story:

> Amber: They (my colleagues) said that if parents learnt more about child development, they'd be more able to participate in what we're doing.

Here is an example of othering from a research study about parent and teacher views of parent involvement in primary schools in the USA (Lawson, 2003):

Some of Garfield's parents perceive this process as a consequence of school staff members viewing themselves as 'experts', thereby ignoring and/ or excluding the opinions of parents. As one involved parent, Rick, noted:

You know, sometimes the teachers be acting like they know about everything on earth, you know, more than you, 'cause they all educated'n stuff. So, you just got to let them think that way until they get to know you. Then they'll listen [laughs]. Well, at least sometimes. (Lawson, 2003:97)

Why othering is unfair

- It promotes being formally educated and the professional, technical language of education this brings as the right way to talk about young children, yet offers no evidence that it is superior to other ways.
- It implies that people who do not use the professional, technical language (jargon) of education and/or are not formally educated do not hold valid views about young children.

How you can counter othering

- Do not assume that there is only one way to talk about young children's education and care.
- Welcome differences in how people talk about early childhood, children, curriculum, and so on.
- Accept that a diversity of views about young children and diverse ways to talk about them is normal and desirable.
- Consider changing your language if it silences, confuses or puzzles the people with whom you are talking.
- Challenge statements that 'other' people who do not use the professional, technical language (jargon) of early childhood.

Points to Ponder

- Before you became involved in early education and care (as a parent, a staff member or a student), how much of your knowledge about young children came from your personal experience? How much came from books, videos, and so on?
- Have you experienced othering (of yourself or of someone else) because of ignorance about (for example) child development?

> **Points to Discuss**
>
> - What have been your most influential sources of knowledge about young children's education and care? What were Amber's (in the story) most influential sources?
> - Does othering do anything more than just point out, 'They're different'?

Models of staff–parent relationships around language

Model 1 is expressed in two quotes chosen from several in an article that presents detailed vignettes of how some staff and parents in the USA negotiate around parents' decisions about their children's education and care (Murray et al., 2007). The quotes recall Amber's conclusion (in the story) that parents and staff have different but equally valuable knowledge about children. Model 2 emerges from a chapter on working with culturally diverse parents in a USA textbook for early childhood professionals about how to build a caring approach to working with parents and communities (McDermott, 2007).

Each model is followed by some 'Points to Ponder' and some 'Points to Discuss', which may help you decide what you think about the relative value of staff's and parents' knowledge and how they express it.

> **Model 1: Parents can express clearly what they want for their children**

> There seem to be choices to make and matters of importance to decide at every turn. At times I feel exhausted from the effort . . . but . . . I still know, without question, that no one else could have made the right choices for our family except our family. (Kathryn Aldridge, parent and co-author). (Murray et al., 2007: 111)

> The vision we have for Bryce is a reflection of our personal value system. The decisions we make on his behalf are guided by that belief system. While professionals do not need to agree with our vision or choices, they must respect them. (Kim Christensen, parent and co-author). (Murray et al., 2007: 111)

> Family choice involves shared responsibility and decision-making power between parents and professionals. When this occurs, families

are empowered and increase their capacity to make informed decisions regarding their child's needs.   (Murray et al., 2007: 111)

> **Model 2: Parents cannot express what they want for their children**

Some parents cannot articulate their goals because they have not thought about their children in those terms, or the stress of daily life has made it difficult for them to focus on goals. However, many parents have never been asked.

(Gross, 1996: 181, cited in McDermott, 2007: 115)

Gross (1986, cited in McDermott, 2007) quoted a study by Taylor et al. (1984), which asked preschoolers' parents what they would like their children to be like in 15 years time. The parents were caught offguard. As Gross explained: 'No-one had ever asked them this question before. Some became tearful, but all were able to describe their hopes for their children's future' (p. 181) (cited in (McDermott, 2007: 115)

Points to Ponder

- Which of the two models of the relationships between professional and non-professional knowledge about young children is closer to yours? Which is closer to Amber's (in the story)?
- Do you agree with Kathryn Aldridge that, 'no one else could have made the right choices for our family except our family'? (Murray et al., 2007) If so, what is the role of professional early childhood expertise?

Points to Discuss

- Does a parent's or carer's choice of an early childhood education and care setting express what they want for their child/ren? Why did Amber (in the story) need to know more about parents' wishes concerning their children?
- In your experience, are all parents as sure of themselves and their wishes for their children as the ones quoted in Model 1?

Further reading to deepen your thinking and talking

Yeun, L. (2009) From foot to shoes: kindergartners', families' and teachers' perspectives of the Project Approach. *Early Childhood Education Journal*, 37(1): 23–33.

Yeun (2009) describes how one early childhood classroom in the USA involved parents as it moved from a theme-based to a project-based curriculum. Parents were given the opportunity to learn about the project-based curriculum and to comment on it. As they learnt more about the project-based curriculum, they engaged critically with it – no longer were they kept at a distance through profession jargon.

Brink, M. (2002) Involving parents in early childhood assessment: perspectives from an early intervention instructor. *Early Childhood Education Journal*, 29(4): 251–7.

Brink (2002) describes how an early intervention professional can involve parents in a developmental assessment of their child. The article includes a list of questions that are notably free of jargon. The questions are asked before, during and after the assessment to ensure that parents can readily express their ideas and views about their children's capacities, growth and learning.

References

Blue-Banning, M., Summers, J., Frankand, H.C., Lord Nelson, L. and Beegle, G. (2004) Dimensions of family and professional partnerships: constructive guidelines for collaboration. *Exceptional Children*, 70(2): 167–84.

Brink, M. (2002) Involving parents in early childhood assessment: perspectives from an early intervention instructor. *Early Childhood Education Journal*, 29(4): 251–7.

Elliott, R. (2003) Sharing care and education: parents' perspectives. *Australian Journal of Early Childhood*, 28(4): 14–21.

Lawson, M. (2003) Family relations in context: parent and teacher perceptions of parent involvement. *Urban Education*, 38(1): 77–133.

McDermott, D. (2007) *Developing Caring Relationships Among Parents, Children, Schools, and Communities*. New York: Sage Publications.

Murray, M., Christensen, K., Umbarger, G., Rade, K., Aldridge, K. and Niemeyer, J. (2007) Supporting family choice. *Early Childhood Education Journal*, 35(2): 111–17.

Sisson, J. (2009) Making sense of competing constructs of teacher as professional. *Journal of Research in Childhood Education*, 23(3): 351–66.

Yeun, L. (2009) From foot to shoes: kindergartners', families' and teachers' perspectives of the project approach. *Early Childhood Education Journal*, 37(1): 23–33.

Appendix 1   A Fairness Alerts Matrix

The Fairness Alerts Matrix provides an overview of each of the unfair thinking habits we use in this book. It can act as a reference tool for further reflection on what unfair thinking habits look and sound like and how you counter them.

Table A.1 A Fairness Alerts Matrix

Unfair thinking habits	How they work	How they look or sound	How you can be fair
Essentializing Seeing an individual as defined by something deep and enduring (essential) because they belong to a particular group (e.g. gender, class, sexuality, language, ethnic or culture). In staff–parent relationships, people may also essentialize each other in terms of whether they have expert knowledge of children.	*`If someone is "X" then – by definition – they act like this, they think like that, and they talk this way. That's just how they are'* *What's unjust about that?* • People are individuals with complex ways of being • Assumptions and stereotypes are often inaccurate • All groups shift and change over time	'Tigers kill – it's what they do' 'Borgs eat greasy food, have loads of children and shout a lot. That's just how they are'	Assume that your assumptions and stereotypes may be inaccurate Be alert to things that you **don't** know about a particular group

Homogenizing Eradicating differences between members of groups (e.g. gender, class, sexuality, language, ethnic or culture) by assuming they do not exist. In staff–parent relationships, people may also homogenize each other in terms of their knowledge, perspectives and experiences as parents or as staff.	`They all think the same way, eat the same things, dress like that, speak that way'* *What's unjust about that?* • People are individuals with complex ways of being • Each group (including yours) has its internal differences, debates, challenges and tensions • Each group (including yours) is diverse and complex	'All tigers are a threat to humanity' 'All Borgs prefer to live together in groups. They do – that's their culture'	Assume that each group may have its own particular internal differences Be alert to signs of differences, debates, challenges and tensions and be prepared to learn about them and from them
Othering Seeing yourself and/or your group as the norm, from which everyone else deviates. In staff–parent relationships, people may also 'other' each other in terms of their knowledge, perspectives and experiences as parents or as staff.	`How those people talk, eat, dress and think is the problem. If only they'd change, we'd get along better'* *What's unjust about that?* • Differences are just/only that – differences	'If the tigers didn't hunt on our land, we wouldn't have to shoot them – we have no choice' 'If Borgs stopped living together in their ghettos, we could understand them better and things wouldn't be so tense'	Assume that differences within and between groups are normal and desirable Be alert to opportunities to change your behaviour if it hurts, harms or offends people in a particular ethnic or cultural group

(Continued)

Table A.1 (*Continued*)

Unfair thinking habits	How they work	How they look or sound	How you can be fair
	• Assuming that how 'we' talk, eat, dress and think is the norm makes everyone else seem strange and exotic • How 'we' talk, eat, dress and think may well offend people in other groups		
Privileging Seeing yourself and/or your group as more important than anyone else. In staff–parent relationships, people may also privilege their group in terms of their perceived greater knowledge and experience because they are a parent or a member of staff.	`We've always done it this way – why should we change just because "X" has happened?'* *What's unjust about that?* • Believing a particular group deserves special treatment just because of who they are • Particular ways of doing things advantage some groups and disadvantage others	'We've lived here for three generations – why should we change just because some tigers have arrived?' 'We've always liked straight talking – why should we change just because the Borg dislike it?'	Assume that each group has an equal right to its ideas, values and way of life Be alert to any inequitable distribution of resources and space between members of particular groups and be prepared to change it

Silencing Making it difficult for an individual or a group to be seen and/or heard. In staff–parent relationships, people may silence each other by preventing each other's experiences, perspectives or knowledge from being expressed, discussed and acted on.	*'This is normal/ right and that's weird/wrong. End of story'* *What's unjust about that?* • To believe that my way is the only way is to dismiss other people by dismissing their points of view.	'The tigers are a threat, so we have to get rid of them, or we'll die' 'The Borg threaten our way of life, so we must stop them moving here'	Assume that each individual or group has valuable ideas and views Be alert to any silencing of an individual or group and actively seek their ideas and views

Appendix 2 Summaries of the major research projects on which the book is based

Parents and professionals in early childhood settings draws on a research programme consisting of three major research projects. Our colleague Dr Kylie Smith was a major contributor to the programme and we are grateful to our research assistants Judy Baird, Anne Farrelly and Melissa Love.

The three major projects are:

1 RESPECT Phase 1. Researching Equitable Staff–Parent Relations in Early Childhood Today, 2005–2006. Victoria, Australia

This small-scale Australian investigation explored staff–parent relations in culturally diverse early childhood communities. The City of Melbourne funded the project. Twelve participants undertook small-scale centre-based action research projects over a twelve-week period, supported by CEIEC researchers Glenda MacNaughton, Kylie Smith and Patrick Hughes. Case studies from the project can be viewed at www.edfac.unimelb.edu.au/ceiec/research/respect/index.html.

2 RESPECT Phase 2. Negotiating Staff–Parent Relations in Culturally Diverse Early Education Settings, 2006–2009. Victoria, South Australia and New South Wales, Australia

This project explored how 60 staff and 60 parents in culturally diverse circumstances understood parent involvement in early education and it examined the forms of knowledge underpinning their current relationships. The Australian Research Council funded this project.

3 Parent Involvement in Early Childhood Services, 2000–2001. Victoria, Australia.

This research study sought to examine staff views on staff–parent relationships, using the model of knowledge-power relationships in staff–parent communication outlined by Hughes and MacNaughton (1999). In

2000, a small, exploratory, qualitative research study aimed at discovering fresh dimensions (Kvale, 1996) on staff–parent relationships was undertaken with 15 early childhood staff in three QIAS-accredited childcare centres in Victoria, Australia. The study addressed two questions: How do these early childhood staff understand and practice parent involvement? How can these understandings be best theorized and related to the international field of early childhood education? The project was funded by Melbourne Research Development Grant, Melbourne International Collaboration Grant.

Parents and professionals in early childhood settings also draws on two action research projects conducted by CEIEC Masters students:

- 'Parent perspectives in early childhood services.' Pat Jewell (Masters of Education)
- 'Linguistic inclusion in early childhood settings.' Prasanna Srinivasan (Masters of Education)

Each project was supervised by Glenda MacNaughton and Margaret Coady.

For additional information about these major projects, please visit the CEIEC website: www.edfac.unimelb.edu.au/CEIEC.

Our research programme has generated several previous publications:

Hughes, P. and MacNaughton, G. (1999) Who's the expert?: reconceptualising staff parent relationships in early childhood. *Australian Journal of Early Childhood*, 24(4): 27–32.

Hughes, P. and MacNaughton, G. (2001) Building equitable staff-parent communication in early childhood settings: an Australian case study. *Early Childhood Research and Practice*, 3(2). Available online at www.ecrp. uiuc.edu/v3n2/hughes.html.

Hughes, P. and MacNaughton, G. (2002) Preparing early childhood professionals to work with parents: the challenges of diversity and dissensus. *Australian Journal of Early Childhood*, 26(4): 32–38.

Hughes, P. and MacNaughton, G. (2006) Whose truth do you privilege? Parents, partnerships and power, in A. Van Keulen (ed.) *Parents and Diversity*. Amsterdam: SWP Publishers.

MacNaughton, G. and Hughes, P. (2000) Consensus, dissensus or community: the politics of parent involvement in early childhood education. *Contemporary Issues in Early Childhood*, 1(3): 241–258.

MacNaughton, G. and Hughes, P. (2003) Curriculum contexts: parents and communities, in G. MacNaughton (ed.) *Shaping Early Childhood: Learners, Curriculum and Contexts*. Maidenhead: Open University Press, pp. 255–81.

MacNaughton, G. and Hughes, P. (2007) Teaching respect for cultural diversity in Australian early childhood programs: a challenge for professional learning. *Journal of Early Childhood Research*, 5(2): 189–204.

Smith, K., MacNaughton, G. and Hughes P. (2005) *Family and Community Partnerships*. CEIEC Members' Briefing Paper, No. 4.2. The University of Melbourne.

Appendix 3 A quick guide to the book's research sources

Table A.3

Chapter	Story	Fairness Alert	Models
1	We/they are always available . . . but in snatches of time	Staff can *silence* parents and vice versa when lack of time makes it difficult for them to communicate effectively with each other	M1: *Time-related problems can be solved through goodwill and some extra effort* M2: *Time-related problems have effects that are inequitable*
2	Understanding the professional	*Privileging* staff's formal, professional knowledge about children in general over parents' informal, anecdotal knowledge about their specific children	M1: *An early childhood curriculum should express teachers' professional knowledge* M2: *An early childhood curriculum should include parents' knowledge about their children*
3	Revealing ignorance	*Silencing* parents by invoking professional knowledge and expertise	M1: *Professional knowledge is messy and uncertain, learnt and unlearnt*

Table A.3 (*Continued*)

Chapter	Story	Fairness Alert	Models
			M2: *Professionals' race and culture can limit or enhance what they know*
4	Joining in – the benefits and costs	*Privileging* staff's professional expertise concerning children in general over parents' knowledge and opinions concerning their specific children	M1: *Parents do not necessarily know how best to help their children's learning* M2: *Parents' knowledge about their children is essential to planning children's learning*
5	We speak English here	Staff can *homogenize* parents and vice versa – 'Oh, they're all like that!' Staff can homogenize parents from diverse backgrounds whom they think are uninvolved in their children's education	M1: *Non-English-speaking parents are uninvolved in their child's education because they regard it as the school's responsibility* M2: *Parental involvement programmes can reproduce existing cultural inequalities*
6	We respect 'their' culture	Parents and staff can *homogenize* each other's culture by thinking, 'They're all like that'	M1: *Culture is a way of seeing the world* M2: *Culture is something to be absorbed*

7	Disclosing personal details – who needs to know?	*Privileging* staff views of what staff need to know about children over the views of parents Privileging the idea that staff have a right to know what children do at home over the idea that families have a right to privacy	M1: *Families have a right to break the 'cycle of silence'* M2: *Families have formal rights to silence*
8	Welcoming parents . . . but not really in this space	*Silencing* parents by having no space for them to talk	M1: *Space can be welcoming and inclusive* M2: *The effects of space can be inequitable*
9	Ways to communicate . . . but don't ruffle their feathers	*Silencing* parents by allowing no views outside the assumed consensus	M1: *Good staff–parent relationships avoid conflict* M2: *Good staff–parent relationships invite difference*
10	I just want some feedback!	*Othering* parents who don't participate	M1: *Staff can motivate parents to get involved in their programme* M2: *Staff cannot motivate parents to get involved in their programme*
11	She'll love the sausage sizzle!	*Privileging* staff's professional expertise concerning children in general over parents' knowledge and opinions concerning their specific children	M1: *Parents' contributions are just add-ons* M2: *Parents' contributions are essential*

(*Continued*)

Table A.3 (*Continued*)

Chapter	Story	Fairness Alert	Models
12	I'm learning how to teach my child to read	*Homogenizing* individuals, families and groups in the same class	M1: *Parents need teachers to tell them how to support their children's literacy* M2: *Teachers can learn from parents how to support young children's literacy*
13	They're just not involved	*Homogenizing* parents who don't meet expectations of 'good' parents	M1: *The more parent involvement, the better* M2: *Parent involvement reflects balance of power in parent–staff relationships*
14	Boys who like to be different	*Essentializing* gender by assuming there are essential ways of being a boy or a girl	M1: *Early childhood education and care staff should initiate provocative discussions about gender equity with parents* M2: *Early childhood education and care staff should be gender equity role models*
15	Lesbian mums: what's the fuss?	*Privileging* heterosexual, two-parent families over any other form of family	M1: *Lesbian and gay families are not normal* M2: *Family diversity is normal*

16	Are we genuine partners and how do we know?	*Silencing* parents' voices in curriculum decision-making	M1: *In genuine partnerships, parents are empowered decision-makers* M2: *In genuine partnerships, parents can have a 'good yack'*
17	That's jargon to me!	*Privileging* professional language as more accurate and valuable than everyday language	M1: *Parents can express clearly what they want for their children* M2: *Parents can't express what they want for their children*

Appendix 4   Handouts for classes, meetings, discussions, newsletters and noticeboards

Parents and professionals in early childhood settings aims to provoke discussion and ideas about how best to create and sustain fair and respectful relationships between staff and parents in early childhood education and care settings. In that sense, the whole book is a 'discussion trigger'. However, this Appendix consists of a series of 'bite–sized' Discussion Triggers that can be used in handouts, questionnaires and surveys, professional development days, classes, meetings, discussions, newsletters and noticeboards to promote active discussion of staff–parent experiences and relationships in early childhood education and care settings.

Each Discussion Trigger draws from the research in this book, is designed with the book's Fairness Alerts in mind and is intended to help staff and parents to create and sustain fair and respectful relationships with each other.

Feel free to use, adapt and circulate the Discussion Triggers as you wish, but please acknowledge their origin.

Discussion Trigger 1: Does everyone have an equal say?

At (your organization), we try to make sure that everyone can have their say and that no one's views and experiences are silenced. Please tell us now what you think about these questions:

- Are there times and spaces when parents and staff can talk privately? Do all parents and staff know about this?
- Is there time and space for informal chats between parents and staff at the start and end of the day?
- If staff and parents speak different languages, is there time for them to share and learn with each other?
- Can you say what you need to say to adults in this centre?

- What is one thing we could do to make sure that everyone gets a say?

Discussion Trigger 2: Learning from each other

A teacher in a US research project said: 'I have no problem with parents participating in my curriculum decisions as long as I make the final decision. Parents can give their opinion but they may not determine what I do' (Addi-Raccah and Arviv-Elyashiv, 2008: 404).

At (your organization), we want things to do things differently. We would like parents and staff to be equal partners in children's learning, so please tell us:

- Do you think that staff–parent partnerships around children's learning is a good idea?
- Would you enjoy being in such a partnership?
- What is one thing we could do to foster staff–parent partnerships?

Research source

Addi-Raccah, A. and Arviv-Elyashiv, R. (2008) Parent empowerment and teacher professionalism: teachers' perspective. *Urban Education*, 43(1): 394–416.

Discussion Trigger 3: Shock! We don't have all the answers

Some early childhood education and care staff believe that for parents and staff to communicate well, they have to build shared understandings about children, which involves each side listening to what the other side says and taking it on board. These staff also believe that if they admit to parents that they do not know all the answers about children, parents will feel more confident to say what they really feel about how they want their children to grow and learn. Please tell us what do you think:

- Do you agree that parents and staff should listen to each other?
- Do you think that staff know all the answers about children?
- What do you think that staff and parents can learn from each other? How can they do so?

Discussion Trigger 4: Joining in – who wins and who loses?

Many people believe that young children do better if their parents or other carers are involved with their kindergarten, childcare, and so on. Involvement can vary between programmes; and parents and carers can differ in whether and how they want to join in their child's programme, depending on their other commitments (e.g. working hours).

At (your organization), we want parents and carers to feel relaxed about joining in our programmes, so please tell us:

- Would you like to participate more or less in our programme?
- If you are participating already, what do you like about being involved in the programme? What makes it hard for you to be involved?
- If you are not participating, would you like to? If you would, what would make it easier for you?

Discussion Trigger 5: News flash – don't ruffle their feathers

A mother whose child was being bullied told researchers that she found it hard to tell her child's primary school teachers that she was concerned. She said: 'You get this very defensive reaction. They don't like, it's almost saying "We don't like you being this articulate and having the knowledge" because they don't have the upper hand' (Vincent and Martin, 2002: 118).

At (your organization):

- Can parents raise hard issues with staff without 'ruffling their feathers?'
- Do staff feel comfortable when 'they don't have the upper hand'?
- What is one thing we could do to make staff and parents more comfortable around hard issues?

Research source

Vincent, C. and Martin, J. (2002) Class, culture and agency: researching parental voice. *Discourse: Studies in the Cultural Politics of Education*, 23(1): 110–28.

Discussion Trigger 6: More information, less jargon, please!

A researcher in Australia found that while parents received written information from staff about their children's programmes, they could not always understand it and there was no follow-up where parents could ask staff to explain what they had written (Elliott, 2003: 18).

At (your organization) we want to be sure that parents and carers know as much as they want to about their children's programmes, so please tell us:

- Is there sufficient written information about the programmes?
- Do we know that everyone understands the written information?
- Should we also provide that information in other forms? Your suggestions, please?

Research source

Elliott, R. (2003) Sharing care and education: parents' perspectives. *Australian Journal of Early Childhood*, 28(4): 14–21.

Discussion Trigger 7: But it's not happening here!

Many people in the early childhood world dislike discrimination against people because of, for example, their gender, ethnicity, class or sexuality; and they believe that early childhood services should promote fairness and equity. However, when a service has no children from groups experiencing discrimination, staff can feel that they do not need to counter discrimination, because 'it's not happening here'.

At (your organization) we want to play our part in promoting fairness and equity and so we want the children to learn about different cultures and ways of life – especially those that they may not encounter locally and that are experiencing discrimination. So please tell us:

- What is one thing that (your organization) can do to promote fairness and equity?
- Can you help to introduce the children at (your organization) to different cultures and ways of life?

Discussion Trigger 8: Keeping it to ourselves

At (your organization) we ask parents and carers for information about children's home life so that there is continuity between how children are looked after at home and here. We realize that some people are cautious about disclosing such personal information, so we have a dilemma: should we risk upsetting parents and carers (a) by asking them about their children's home life or (b) by looking after their children differently than they do at home?

Please help us to resolve this dilemma!

- If you are a parent or carer, what would you like to say about your child's home life?
- If you are a staff member (or a student on placement), what do you need to know in order to look after children appropriately?

Appendix 5 Glossary of key terms

Parents and professionals in early childhood settings draws on research about staff–parent relationships from several different countries. The language used to describe early childhood education and care services varies between countries and the same word (e.g. 'kindergarten') can refer to services for children between three and eight years of age and its meaning can differ between countries. This glossary provides a broad guide to the different terms used to refer to the services for children between birth and eight years of age in the different countries from which we have drawn research and to the staff that provide them.

- **Childcare services** provide non-parental care for children between 0 and 5 years of age.
- **Children's services** is used in Australia to refer to services provided for children outside of formal schooling. It includes, **preschools, childcare services, family day care** and **out-of-school hours care**.
- **Early childhood** is defined by the United Nations and accepted internationally as the period between conception and eight years of age. As such, it includes a child's early years in primary education.
- **Early childhood education and care** is used in several countries (e.g. Australia and New Zealand) to refer to educational services for young children. They may be delivered at home, at a hospital or at a centre.
- **Early childhood educators** is used in several countries (e.g. Australia and New Zealand) to refer to people who work with children between birth and eight years old in a care and/or education setting such as an early years service or the early years of compulsory schooling. An early childhood educator may or may not have formal tertiary early childhood qualifications.

- **Early childhood services** or **early childhood education and care services** are care and education services for children between birth and eight years old and their families. The range of services differs between countries.
- **Early Learning Centre** refers (in Australia) to an educational service for young children in their years before formal schooling. An Early Learning Centre is often attached to a school.
- **Elementary school** is used in the USA to refer to a child's first formal school.
- **Family day care** means different things in different countries. In Australia, it refers to home-based, non-parental care services; in the UK, it means childminding; and in the USA, it refers to home-based care.
- **Head Start** is a programme in the USA for children aged between three and four years old from low-income families, funded by the federal government.
- **Heteronormative** is a negative bias against same-sex sexual relationships and a positive bias towards opposite-sex sexual relationships that promotes these opposite-sex sexual relationships as normal.
- **Heterosexism** is institutional and personal discrimination, bias and prejudice against lesbians or gay men that priveleges heterosexuals and implies that heterosexuality is normal.
- **Homophobia** is a hatred, fear and/or contempt for people who are homosexual.
- **Kindergarten** is used differently between countries and, sometimes, within a country. For example, in some states in Australia, kindergarten refers to the first year of school, but in the Australian state of Victoria, it refers to an educational service for children in the year preceding school. In the USA and in Anglophone Canada, kindergarten often refers to a five-year-old child's first year of school. In Israel, kindergartens are part of the preschool system, but in Germany, kindergartens provide care and education services for children up to six years old and are part of the social welfare system. In Denmark and Finland, a kindergarten year is optional for children between 6 and 7 years old. The kindergarten year is often seen as preparing children for school and focuses on children's social and emotional development.
- **Long day care** is a non-parental care service generally for children between 0 and 5 years of age.
- **Model** is a generalized picture of something (e.g. relationships between parents and staff), through which specific instances are

understood. It is not necessarily true – it is just one understanding – so there may be more than one model of something.

- **Nursery school** is used in the UK to refer to preschool education for children over three years old.
- **Occasional care** services are often provided for children under five years of age in a children's centre on an hourly or sessional basis.
- **Practicum** is used in Australia to refer to supervised placement of students in early childhood services. It is sometimes also referred to as field work.
- **Preschool** is a term that is used differently in different countries. For instance, in Australia and New Zealand, preschool is synonymous with **kindergarten**. In the USA, preschool is often used to refer to childcare centres that care primarily for children aged between three and four years old. A preschool can be based in a centre, a family childcare home or a public school.
- **Reggio Emilia** system of (or approach to) early childhood education developed by Loris Malaguzzi (1920–1994) in the Emilia-Romagna region of northern Italy.
- **SES** is the abbreviated form of **socio-economic status**.
- **Socio-economic status** (**SES**) is a synonym of class or social class.
- **Special education** is used in the USA and in some other countries to refer to educational services that include specialist support to children with a disability or developmental delay and to their families.
- **Sure Start** is a programme in the UK in which children's centres provide integrated childcare, early education, health and family support services between 8.00 a.m. and 6.00 p.m. for children in the years before compulsory schooling.

Index

Advantaged, 89

Barriers, 56, 104–106, 109, 112, 115, 141
Bilingual, 48, 50–52, 54, 55–56
Bisexual, 171, 172

CEIEC, vi, 202, 203, 204
Co-construction, 34, 45, 100
Collaborating, 37
Collaboration, vii, 43, 140, 176, 189, 196
Collaborators, 15, 128
Collectivism, 62, 63, 66
Confidential, 70, 75
Confidentiality, 70, 76, 77, 78, 79, 80
Consensus, ix, xii, 63, 93, 97–99, 207
Critical conversations, 96
Cultural differences, 64
Cultural diversity, 58, 134, 135, 170
Cultural inequality, 55
Culture – definition, 64
Culture – dominant, 72
Culture – models, 64–66
Culture – school, 59, 62
Cultures and language, 135
Cycle of silence, 77, 78, 207

Decision-making, 145, 178, 181, 194, 209
Democratic, 77
Dialogical, 100
Dilemma/s, 75, 91, 102, 126, 214
Disability, 79, 217
Disadvantaged, 6, 10, 60, 89, 126–130,
   130–131
Discussion triggers, 210–214
Diversity – cultural, 58, 91, 134–135, 170,
   204
Diversity – ethnic, 61
Diversity – family, 160–162, 169, 170, 208
Diversity – linguistic, 9, 136
Diversity and dissensus, xii

Early childhood educators, 22, 215
English language learners, 48, 52, 56
Essentialist, 56, 61

Essentializing – countering, 155
Essentializing – definition, 153
Essentializing – examples, 154
Essentializing – unfairness, 155, 198
Ethical dilemmas, 101, 102
Ethnicity, 30, 52, 58, 62, 109, 153
Experts, literacy, 128
Experts, parents as, 19, 42
Experts, staff as, 15, 24, 69, 118, 138, 192

Fairness Alerts Matrix, v, xi, 198–201
Family participation, vii, 89
First Nations, 114–115, 123

Gay, 148–156, 160–161, 164–172, 208, 216
Gender equity, 148, 150–152, 156–159, 208
Gender issues, 150
Gender policies, 157–158
Gender values, 157

Head Start, 25, 34, 104–106, 216
Heterosexism, 161
Heterosexuality, 161, 165, 216
Homogeneous, 98
Homogenizing – countering, 53, 63, 131,
   144
Homogenizing – definition, 52, 62, 130,
   142, 199
Homogenizing – examples, 52, 62, 130,
   142–143
Homogenizing – unfairness, 53, 63, 131,
   143
Homophobia, 161, 169, 216

Immigrant, 56, 62–67, 72, 75, 143, 147
Inclusive, 46, 88, 100, 162, 168, 171
Individualism, 62, 63, 66
Information evenings, 16
Information sharing, 78, 181
Involvement, family, vii, 26–34, 43–45,
   108, 123, 147

Knowledge, anecdotal, 17, 19, 119, 205
Knowledge, expert, 18, 198

Knowledge, funds of, 32
Knowledge, hierarchy of, 7, 17, 179
Knowledge, indigenous, 19–22, 47, 63
Knowledge, parents', 37, 40, 41, 43, 206
Knowledge, scientific, 17, 39
Knowledges, 34

Language – othering, 192
Languages, 47–48, 51–54, 56, 135, 210
Lesbian, 160–172, 208, 216
Little narratives, ix
Looping, 10–11

Mainstream, 8, 29, 64–65, 92–93, 97–99, 180
Middle class, 32, 61, 95, 112, 131, 162
Middle class families, 44, 55, 151, 170

Non-involvement, 55
Normality, 169
Normative, 61

Othering – countering, 133, 168, 193
Othering – definition, 108
Othering – examples, 108, 132, 167, 192
Othering – unfairness of, 109, 133, 168, 193
Othering and homogenizing, 21, 130
Othering and privileging, 165, 190

Paradigm, 33, 34, 172
Parent information forms, 69,75
Parent involvement programs, 55, 175
Parent involvement, childcare, 123–124
Parent involvement, early childhood education, xii, 116, 118, 120, 202–203
Parent involvement, school, 56, 60–61, 115, 139, 192
Parent involvement, survey, 105
Parent participation, 41, 146, 147, 181
Parents' room, 85
Parents' views, 15, 17, 41–44, 87, 147, 178
Personal information, 69, 72, 76, 79, 214
Politics, cultural, 15, 22, 102, 162, 172, 212
Politics, emotional, 15, 22, 162, 172
Poststructuralism, x, 31
Power relations, 14, 82, 202
Powerlessness, 55, 78, 162
Practicum, 12, 217

Privacy, 14, 69, 74–78, 207
Privileging – countering, 18, 41, 76, 119, 166, 191
Privileging – definition, 17, 40, 74, 118, 165, 190
Privileging – examples, 17, 40, 74–75, 118–119, 165–166, 191
Privileging – unfairness, 17, 41, 76, 119, 166, 191
Provoke, ix, 156–158, 210

Race, 32, 41, 58, 66, 153, 206
Racial group, 53, 63, 144
Regio Emilia, 25–26, 34, 191, 217
Religion, 37, 163, 170
Right to know, 74, 77, 80

Sexuality, 148, 153, 160–161, 168–169, 198–199, 213
Silencing – countering, 7, 87, 98, 179
Silencing – definition, 6, 28, 86, 97, 178
Silencing – examples, 6–7, 28, 86, 97, 178
Silencing – unfairness, 7, 29, 87, 98, 179
Single parent, 75, 79, 89, 100, 170
Social justice, 90
Socialization, racial, 32
Socio-economic status, 83, 93, 101, 106, 131, 217
Special education, 20, 217
Staff-child ratios, 72, 82
Stereotypes, 61, 95–99, 108–110, 152–156, 161, 169, 198
Stories, traditional, 20
Student conferences, 16

Technical language, 192–193
Time related problems, 9, 205
Time, scarce, 6–10
Transgendered, 171, 172

Uncertainty, viii, 25, 31–34, 65
Uninvolved, 52–54, 106–110, 144, 206
Unprofessional, 26, 69

Welcoming, 51, 81–89, 207
Working class, 93, 150

Yacking, 181–182
Yarnin', 77–80